Principles
For
Principals

Lessons I Learned Along the Way

Jerry Schiffman

Jerry Schiffman

Thanks to:

Pete My Pusher

Harriet My Finisher

And a special thanks to

My Favorite Assistant

Dubba

Copyright @ 2012 Jerry Schiffman

ISBN-13: 978-1470094386

ISBN-10: 147009438X

Introduction

This began as just a recalling of stories, some funny and some serious, that I have experienced through the years. Each gave me a little more insight into the impact a teacher or principal has on people, be they students, parents, fellow teachers or fellow principals. I would tell these stories at luncheons or gatherings and was encouraged to write them down so that others could enjoy them and learn from them. As a Principal, I always consider myself a teacher of teachers. I think the incidents related in this book have each contributed to my experience in carrying out that task.

Teaching children is one of the most rewarding, interesting, challenging and difficult jobs there is. After a lifetime of getting up in the morning and going to school as a student, or teacher or principal I realize how much of an affect teachers have had on my life. I take them all seriously.

The military taught me that everyone in the army was in support of the soldier who was delivering the service. Therefore, all efforts should be focused on helping the deliverer of that service. I carried that thought with me as the Principal of a school. It is the classroom teacher who delivers the service. Everyone must be in support of their efforts in order to assist them in fulfilling the goals set for them.

The job taught me that I would have to make many decisions each day. Most were easy, some were hard, but all had to be made. There were issues that were very controversial. It was not unusual to have two diametrically opposed solutions offered for consideration. Both sides were absolutely sure that they were correct and the other was wrong.

It was most important that both sides knew that I had taken their suggestions seriously. In making the decision, my first consideration was always the welfare of the students. Second was how it would affect the staff and third was what impact, if any, it had on the rest of the school. When it was clear in my mind that my decision was in the best interest of those considerations, the decision was easy and I was comfortable making it.

Frank McCourt wrote a book entitled "Teacher Man", in which he describes the wonderful stories that he experienced as a teacher at the secondary level. This book contains some wonderful stories experienced by me at the elementary level. It is amazing how similar many of the stories are.

Table of Contents

Chapter 1

Communication

Communication: that illusive ability to transfer ones thoughts to others in a manner that is understood by both. What you say may not always be what others hear! Check for these three parts: information, transmission and reception.

Head Lice:

Some years ago, head lice came to my school on Long Island. Most of us had not dealt with this problem before. We soon learned about Quell, nits, and panic. Some parents volunteered to help while others were reluctant even to send their children to school. The school nurse and a small group of PTA volunteers spent days checking heads and phoning parents to tell them to take their child home and what to do for them when they got home.

The PTA president was very supportive. She did her best to calm parents who would call her to vent their anger or ask questions. One day she came to my office to talk about strategy. She asked me how things were going. I was pleased to tell her that as of that day we were down to only two cases. She looked at me quizzically. "Why would you have any cases?" she said. Now I was quizzical. "Well, the Nurse has been working very hard and she told me yesterday that at last count that is what we had." She became a little agitated and continued to ask, "Why?" Slowly I began to realize that in her mind she was visualizing *crates* of lice. When I said, "cases" she thought boxes.

Communication! I laughed out loud! Can you visualize these little critters running around in a box? She was embarrassed and I promised that I would tell the story but I would never mention her name. The incident remains with me to this day. It has made me listen to what I say with an ear for how it could be misinterpreted.

"We Gonna"

As hard as it can be to communicate when both parties speak the same language, things really get interesting when neither speaks the other's language.

One Friday afternoon Mrs. Augusta and her six-year old daughter appeared at the counter of the outer office. They had just come to this country from Italy and neither could speak English. Someone must have told Mrs. Augusta about registering her daughter Theresa for school because she brought all the necessary papers.

I overheard my secretary struggling to get more information from our prospective client. She was not getting very far so she turned the problem over to me. I smiled and introduced myself. Mrs. Augusta smiled back and pointed to the papers. I looked at the birth certificate and realized that Theresa was six and chronologically eligible for the first grade but it seemed to me that her language needs would be better served in our Half-Day Kindergarten program. How to tell her?

Just then, Mr. De Angelo, our Italian custodian, came walking down the hall. Providence had smiled on me! Mr. De Angelo's English was not that good but his Italian was perfect for what was needed.

I asked Mr. De Angelo to please translate for me and tell Mrs. Augusta that we would prefer to place Theresa in a Kindergarten where her language needs would be better served.

Mr. De Angelo began speaking in beautiful Italian. Mrs. Augusta smiled and nodded. Great! They were "communicating". He went on for many minutes and I started getting worried about what else he might be saying. I tried to interject but he assured me that it was going well. I let them finish.

At the end, we registered Theresa in Kindergarten. "Good job Jerry." I talk to myself on occasion. "You used another school resource." That afternoon I left school feeling happy and ready to spend the weekend with my family.

Monday morning brought a very excited Mrs. Augusta to the front office. As soon as I heard her voice, I knew who it was. Mrs. Augusta made it clear that she was not happy with the Half-Day Kindergarten, half-day being the problem. Holding up the papers we gave her on Friday she repeated, "No good, no good!" I wanted to neither reason with her nor deny her request, but how could I tell her that we would reregister Theresa in a first grade?

Again, I looked for Mr. De Angelo but he was nowhere to be found. Instead, fortune brought me Margaret Di Toronto. There's the vowel I was looking for. I beckoned for Margret to come into the office and I explained the problem and the solution. The following conversation transpired:

Me: "Margaret, I need to have you tell Mrs. Augusta that we will put Theresa in a first grade as she is requesting."

Margaret: "Jerry, I don't speak Italian."

Me: "I'm not asking for a complicated discussion. All I need is for her to know we agree with placing Theresa in a first grade."

Margaret: A bit vexed "I cannot even do that, I don't speak Italian."

Me: A little louder "Did your father and mother come from Italy?"

Margaret: "Yes"

Me: "Then you must know something! Do the best you can."

Margaret, turning toward Mrs. Augusta and with her thumb, fore finger and middle finger facing upward and touching, began speaking very slowly and louder than necessary: "Mrs. Augusta, we 'gonna' put Theresa in the prima grade."

I nearly lost it right there. I thought that even I knew that much Italian. The best is that Mrs. Augusta understood what Margaret said and went away happy.

Communication had taken place.

John and His Prosthesis:

Get the word out to everyone who needs to know. If you don't, the person who needed to know could be in big trouble!

One day during the summer, Mrs. Finley came to school to register her son John for Kindergarten. She asked to speak to me and was ushered into my office. I knew Mrs. Finley because she had three other children attending our school. After the usual greetings, she introduced me to John her cute little five-year-old, blue-eyed son. "John" she said, "is a Thalidomide baby and was born with an incomplete right leg." With that, John reached down and removed the prosthesis that served as his right leg. His leg ended just below the knee. The prosthesis was cone shaped and had a shoe at the end of it that matched his other shoe. He slipped it back on as naturally as putting on a slipper and stood up to show me how he could walk. The only person more cool about this than Mrs. Finley was John. Mrs. Finley explained that John was very well adjusted. She wanted the teachers and staff to know about it but she didn't want anyone to make a fuss about it. I agreed and she and John left.

Now to inform the staff! I set about preparing a memo that contained the information Mrs. Finley and I had discussed. Then I sent copies to everyone I could think of who might come into contact with John. That included the other Kindergarten teachers, the special teachers, art, physical education, music, the nurse, the custodians, the cafeteria people and the secretaries. A copy was safely placed into each of their mailboxes with a RSVP confirmation.

The summer ended and school started on a Wednesday. In my walk around I made a special stop in the Kindergarten class and saw that John was doing fine.

That Friday things changed drastically. Suddenly I heard screams coming from the Kindergarten room that was just down the hall. I rushed down to see what was happening and witnessed the following scene:

John was sitting on the floor putting his prosthesis back on. Mrs. Martin, the substitute music teacher was hysterical as she stood staring at John as John replaced his leg. She was shaking uncontrollably! I called the teacher's room and had the Kindergarten teacher return to her class so that I could remove the hysterical Mrs. Martin from the classroom.

Once in my office, Mrs. Martin began to calm down. I asked her what had happened. With a halting voice, she related the following. She was teaching rhythm and how there is a steady beat to the music. The children were clapping their hands to the beat. Some children could not get the rhythm so Mrs. Martin had them sit on her lap. She tapped out the beat by bouncing the child on her knee. It was John's turn to sit on Mrs. Martin's lap. Mrs. Martin bounced John up and down on her lap in time to the music. The bouncing loosened John's prosthesis and it fell to the floor with a thud. Mrs. Martin looked down at the leg and the rest you can imagine. I don't think Mrs.

Martin ever recovered nor did she ever forgive me for her not knowing about John's leg.

The problem was that Mrs. Martin was a substitute and was not in the loop for my memo. Substitute teachers are part of the group that needed to know!

"Who Needs To Know" is the operative phrase!

Chapter 2

Parents: Some Angry, Some Funny

No matter how you try and how good you are, there will come a day when a parent will disagree with your decision and you will be unable to quell their anger. I try to remain calm in my responses. Parents have every right to disagree with any decision I have made. They have every right to know the facts that went into my making the decision. If they convinced me that they were right and I was wrong, I would say so and change. However, if they became abusive or they could not be convinced and persisted I would finally say, "When you are the Principal of this school you can make the decisions." Please use this as a last resort to end the discussion! Or maybe it is better to never use it.

The Balabusta

Every principal has experienced the mother who is over protective of her child. She comes to school for every little incident and blows the issue out of proportion. But she has the right to be heard.

Mrs. C was one of those. In fact, she became known to me on the very first day of school. In order to get her daughter into the Kindergarten classroom I had to peel her off her mother's leg as she screamed and held on tight. I was finally half way to the room when Mrs. C stopped me and asked if she could just give her daughter one more hug. I knew this was going to be trouble. That hug started the entire problem over again. Finally, I was able to tear her away from the clutches of her mother and assure Mrs. C that everything would be all right.

After a half hour, I visited the classroom to see Mrs. C's daughter playing nicely with a classmate. I returned to my office and telephoned Mrs. C to tell her all was well. She expressed her appreciation.

From that first day on Mrs. C found reasons to charge up to school. If records were kept for things like this, she would have been the champ. But our story takes place years later. Her daughter was now in the third grade. I heard Mrs. C's familiar voice in the outer office. She was highly agitated. Most of the time, my wonderful secretaries could calm her down and resolve the issue. Not this time! She insisted on seeing me. My secretary, Mrs. Tardio came to my door, rolled her eyes and said, "Mrs. C insists on seeing you."

I'll spare you the entire interchange and just relate the essentials.

Mrs. C: "I want a new teacher for my daughter."

Me: What happened?

Mrs. C: "That teacher embarrassed my daughter yesterday in front of the whole class and now she doesn't want to go to school."

Me: "Let me check with the teacher."

I went to the classroom and got the story. The class was doing a unit on nutrition and in particular, healthy snacks. The children were to bring a snack to school the next day, read the ingredients and tell why it was a healthy snack. Her daughter brought a container of Chocolate Pudding. It was one of those food products that was loaded with sugar and chemicals whose names could not even be pronounced. The rest of the children brought fruit or carrots. When her daughter told the class what she brought the kids ganged up on her telling her that "Chocolate Pudding was not a healthy snack!"

I returned to my office to continue my visit with Mrs. C. The Following is a synopsis of our conversation.

Me: "Mrs. C, this was a lesson about nutrition and eating healthy snacks and food. It culminated in the children bringing healthy snacks to school. Your daughter brought chocolate pudding that was loaded with sugar. Not exactly a healthy snack!"

Mrs. C calmed down and explained, "I didn't know about the lesson and I didn't have anything else in the house. But Mr. Schiffman, I want you to know that people consider me a Balabusta!"

Now Balabusta is a Yiddish term for a woman who is an outstanding mother and homemaker. Not many Jews let alone non-Jews know its meaning. That broke the ice. I laughed and asked her if she knew what a Balabusta was? She told me she lived among Jews and knew many Yiddish words. We both laughed and the problem was settled. There's nothing like humor to resolve issues.

After she left, I told Lucy what Mrs. C said about being a "Balabusta" and what it meant. Mrs.Tardio said, "You got it wrong, she is a Ball-a-Buster." (Sorry for needing to use that language but it is a direct quote!)

After that, we would characterize the people who constantly complained as Balabustas.

The Husband's Telephone Call

It was 7:00 in the morning. I had gotten to work early so that I could get some work done on my "To Do" list that was weeks old. The phone rang. Ordinarily I would not answer it this early, (our day started at 8:00) but I was expecting a call. It was not the call I expected. On the other end of the phone was a very angry man who was being prompted in the background by his wife. The conversation went something like this:

Husband: (In a strong voice) "I understand you have not yet resolved the problem with regard to the best reading group for my daughter."

Me: "Sir, I spoke to the reading teacher and she has set up an appointment to test your child this week. That will help us determine the group best suited for her."

Husband: (In a softer voice) "Oh I see."

Wife: (In the background in a loud whisper) "What do you mean, I'll see. Ask him when they will make the change."

I'll spare you the details by just saying that the conversation of husband to me to wife to husband to me went on for quite a while. Every time he was satisfied with my answer, she would prod him to get tougher. He sounded increasingly conflicted as the conversation went on. I realized his predicament and after quite a few minutes I said, "I realize that your wife is very frustrated and angry and won't be satisfied until you let me have it. So, feel free to raise your voice and tell me off and hang up." I don't know what made me say that but it just felt right.

There was silence for a few seconds. Then, raising his voice to an angry pitch, he told me off and warned me to get the situation fixed! Then he hung up the phone. I smiled and figured I did a good deed.

Now for the best part of the story! Two hours later, my secretary told me that the husband was on the phone and wanted to talk to me. For a second I wondered if I had misread the situation and really overstepped the bounds. Nevertheless, I had not. He called me from his office to thank me for understanding the spot he was in and for giving him the way out. We laughed about it and recounted the phone conversation for several minutes. He became my forever friend. He came to the next few PTA meetings and just made eye contact with me and we smiled.

Mrs. E and "No Call Until Christmas"

Mrs. E was the most difficult parent I, or any of my staff, ever had to deal with. She could call me or her daughter's teacher 3 or 4 times a day. Once on the phone it was next to impossible to end the conversation without being rude. She would also call board members, the Superintendent and once even a United State Senator. Yes, a United State Senator. She complained about everything from the bus ride to the cafeteria food and noise, the teacher's method of teaching and many other issues. This began in Kindergarten and continued through the grades.

I tried many ways to get Mrs. E to say what she wanted to say, hear my responses and get off the phone, but nothing could stop her. She would just repeat the same thing over and over again until my patience ran out and I couldn't stand it any longer. I would tell her I was late for a meeting and hang up.

On one of these occasions, I guess I hung up too abruptly. The next thing I knew the Superintendent called me to ask if I had indeed hung up on this woman. I said, "Yes, I had" and then explained the situation saying that I had the rest of the school to run and I could not give this woman the hours each day that would satisfy her. He accepted my explanation but cautioned me to have more patience. Well, now that she had the Superintendent's ear she began calling him frequently.

Weeks went by when one day I got a call from the Superintendent. He said, "Jerry, I want you to know that I just hung up on Mrs. E." We laughed for a long time as he related some of the details of his phone call conversations with Mrs. E. He totally understood the problem.

But the story goes on. Mrs. E's daughter was in second grade. It was early in the school year and I had already logged many calls from Mrs. E. In an effort to shorten the calls, I told her she could only call me with one topic and she had to stick to that one topic. That worked for a while until the time we finished one conversation and she hung up only to call again minutes later with her second complaint.

On this particular occasion, I had arranged a meeting with Mr. and Mrs. E. along with the classroom teacher, the reading teacher, the psychologist, the nurse and me. We outlined the plan we had all agreed would help their daughter with her learning problems. Mr. E gently explained the plan to Mrs. E. I took note of how he spoke to her as if she were a child. She listened carefully and nodded. Mr. and Mrs. E. seemed very happy with the plan. We agreed to implement the plan starting the following Monday. Fine!

On that Monday, we launched the plan. At 1:30 that afternoon, Mrs. E. called to ask how the plan was working. I started to get upset but then I remembered how Mr. E spoke to her at the meeting and instead of getting angry I told her we had started the plan and that she was not to call me until Christmas and then to wish me a happy New Year. She said "Okay." We said goodbye and hung up. Was this really going to work?

Months went by with no calls from Mrs. E. Had I finally succeeded in finding a way to solve the problem. Just give her a direct order in a quiet voice! The phone rang one day. It was the assistant superintendent. He said, "Jerry, I just got a very strange phone call from a Mrs. E. She complained that someone kicked her daughter's lunch box and broke it. I told her to call you but she said she was not allowed to call you until Christmas." I couldn't stop laughing long enough to tell him the story. It took many minutes for me to gain enough composure to explain the reasons.

There were dozens of stories attributed to Mrs. E, but let me just say that after a few years we became good friends. We finally worked out a way to deal with problems that satisfied both our needs.

The Done Deal

There's no better way to get a faculty behind the principal than for the principal to show support for a deserving teacher.

Helen was a second year, third grade teacher who was eager to learn her craft. She was very traditional in her methods and got good results on test scores. She came to my office one day to ask me to help her set up an integrated unit. She had heard from other teachers on her grade level how much they enjoyed doing an integrated learning project with their students and she was ready to try one. We talked about the various topics that would lend themselves to an interesting unit and settled on one that involved breakfast cereal and the importance of good nutrition.

Ideas were discussed and a plan developed whereby the students would conduct a survey of the various cold cereals that they most commonly ate. They would check the ingredients written on each package for their nutritional value and compare that to what was considered to be a healthy product. They would make charts and take surveys of their favorite cereal. The survey could include the rest of the classes on their grade level. The art and music teachers were informed so that they could gear their lessons to the project. The ideas grew so that the unit included all the aspects of the curriculum. Reading, writing, arithmetic, art, and music were easily plugged into the lessons. Students learned to work cooperatively using their imagination to produce their final project. Letters were sent home explaining the project so that the parents could be involved if they wished.

The unit had been going on for more than a week when Helen came to my office with a letter that she held in her hand. She had tears in her eyes as she told me it was from a parent who was very critical of what she was doing with the class and his child in particular.

I read the letter that was signed by Mr. Z and I understood why Helen was almost in tears. It was the nastiest letter I had read in a long time. Mr. Z was the Principal of a nearby elementary school and obviously was very opposed to any integrated learning unit work. In his letter, he stated that it wasted the time of the students and did not prepare them for the tests they would be taking.

It is perfectly okay for anyone to express an opinion and even object to this approach, but the way Mr. Z did it was vicious. His language was accusatory, denunciative and attacking. He went on at length about how poorly she taught and what he would do if she taught in his school. At the end of the letter, he demanded a meeting with her.

I was as upset as Helen was after reading the letter. I told her that he had way over stepped the boundary of decency and used his Principal's title to intimidate her. She was afraid to meet with him alone so I recommended they meet together with me in my office. I assured her the meeting would be cordial! Helen felt a lot better about that.

She informed Mr. Z of the time and place for the meeting. He objected to this and called to speak to me directly. He was very upset about having to meet with the teacher in my office with me present. I explained that it was my decision and that it was not negotiable. He was livid and used a curse word to show his anger. I stopped him and told him I did not tolerate listening to that kind of language. He sarcastically asked if I had never heard that word before. I told him that I would not speak to him if he persisted in that tone. He persisted and I hung up.

Moments later I heard the outer office phone ring and my secretary told me he was on the phone. I took the call and told him that I had hung up and if he used that language again, I would hang up and not accept calls from him. That stopped him. We set up the appointment.

When the day came, I was ready. I felt like a matador waiting for the bull to enter the ring. I set the chairs so that he would be sitting at one end of the table, Helen and I at the other. I held his letter in front of me.

He began to tell his story and what his objections were. He was upset because he thought that unit work was just for fun and that his daughter would not learn the curriculum for the grade using that method. When he paused, waiting for me to reply, I looked at him and remained silent for many seconds. You could feel the tension in the room. I just remained silent waiting for him to finish. After a few long seconds of silence, he continued with his tirade. After a few of these calculated pauses, I asked if he was finished. He sat back and said "yes."

I then asked Helen to show him how the lessons included the teaching of the curriculum in writing, reading, math, spelling, science and health. He started to interject a comment but I reminded him that we did not interrupt him when he spoke and expected him to show the same courtesy. Helen showed Mr. Z the numerous skills she would be teaching and the research that students had to do in order to gather information about their topic. She explained that as a culminating activity each student had to prepare to present his or her information to the class.

At the end, Mr. Z was still not convinced but at least he behaved more like a gentleman. Helen returned to her class. I asked Mr. Z to remain for a few minutes so that we could clear up our issues. I asked if we could talk as man-to-man rather than parent-to-principal. He reluctantly agreed. I explained that the nastiness of his letter was why I intervened to protect Helen from him and told him how important it was for him to learn this lesson if he ever expected to be a successful Principal. We disagreed about many issues but he left understanding that it was my responsibility to support my staff and to not allow anyone to intimidate any one of them. It would be a good lesson for him to learn.

The best part of this entire episode is that my support for Helen was all over the school. Teachers who often hear the words from principals about standing up for teachers saw it by my action. No claims of being supportive of teachers could have meant as much to the staff as what they heard.

The Parent Observation

My first two years of teaching were with an outstanding Principal, who really respected his teachers and had their respect as well. I learned a lot in those two years due to his leadership and a wonderful, helping staff. After a year and three months of teaching, I was drafted and I spent the next 21 months and a day in the United States Army.

After being discharged, I returned to the district hoping to restart my teaching career. There was no opening at my old school so I was assigned to a new building with a different Principal who I shall call Mrs. Y. I was given a great 5th grade class in this affluent neighborhood and I enjoyed teaching them.

One day the mother of one of my students came to my classroom and asked to sit in on my class. In fact, she said, "My son has been telling me how much he is enjoying school this year and since I have no other plans today I wonder if I could sit in on your class?"

I was not expecting this but after a moment's thought, I said I didn't think it would be a good idea. Her son was not "one of the boys" in the class that the other boys liked. In fact, in the beginning of the year they often picked on him. I had been working on improving the situation with him and the rest of the boys and it was getting better. I told her that her being there could embarrass her son and make the other children feel uncomfortable.

She looked shocked! "You mean you won't let me?" I guess she was not expecting to be refused and she showed me her anger. She walked off in a huff. What I didn't know was that she went directly to the principal's office with her request. I found out when she returned with a note signed by the principal telling me to allow her to visit and watch my lesson. I was very upset. She didn't even check with me as to my reasons for the denial.

The day began and I was mulling the situation over in my mind. I was really bothered by the whole thing. But then a thought entered my mind and I knew what I was going to say. I was able to relax and teach the class. Lunchtime came and the parent came over to thank me and said, "I really enjoyed your lessons and I know now why my son loves to come to school."

That should have satisfied me but I was still upset with being preempted and overruled. Without thinking it through, I thanked her for the compliment and went on to say, "I have a PTA meeting tonight and I have nothing to do after school until the meeting. Would you mind if I came to your house this evening and watched you prepare dinner?"

She did not think that was funny and coming from a lowly teacher she was insulted. She went directly back to the principal and complained about my remark. I received a pretty good tongue-lashing but that's okay!

Some things are worth being reprimanded for.

Say "Yes" With a Smile

I learned this valuable lesson in a very unusual way but it has stayed with me for all these years. As a male 5th grade teacher, I received more after-shave lotion and men's cologne from the students each year than I could ever use in a lifetime. Each year I would thank the kids for their thoughtfulness and pack the items in a box that I stored in the garage.

One day while browsing in a department store that serviced our area, I noticed that all the brands of cologne and lotion were sold in this department. I went up to the salesperson and explained that I had scores of unopened bottles of the products he sold. Then I asked him if I could exchange some of them for other items he carried that I could use. He started asking me for receipts. Of course, I had none and explained that these were presents from the kids.

He then asked how I knew that they were purchased in his department. I explained that the school was very near to this store and I was fairly sure that their parents would have shopped here.

He went on to come up with other less significant reasons for not making the exchange. I thanked him anyway and was about to leave when he started to change his mind. He finally agreed to my returning a dozen items. I thanked him and rushed home to bring the items back to him.

When I returned he went back to telling me why he should not do this. I just waited silently as he continued to complain about the deal we had made. I returned the dozen unusable items and chose the items that I could use. As he packed the items he continually grumbled, letting me know this was not his usual practice.

I took the items, thanked him again and left. All the way home, I thought about what had happened. I was able to exchange some items, but the salesperson left me with little gratitude toward him or the store. I realized then that if I was eventually going to agree to do something, even something that I was not happy about, I would do it with a smile so that I could at least get some benefit from it.

If you know you are going to say "Yes", say it with a smile!

Asbestos and Smoking

One day, just like the sudden appearance of head lice, asbestos hit the news. Someone found that schools, as well as other facilities, used asbestos to cover pipes in order to keep the water hot that heated the rooms at the far end of the building. There is no doubt that asbestos, once thought of as the best method for covering pipes, was found to be a very dangerous material. Though asbestos was used in many places, schools were targeted by the media. Whenever there are children involved in a dangerous situation the media is all over it, as they should be.

We were besieged with worried parents who went to Board of Education meetings and wanted answers about their concerns for the safety of their children. The BOE contracted with specialists who measured the amount of asbestos in the air in each classroom. They found some but far less than what was considered to exceed unsafe limits. Even the small amount was not what the parents wanted to hear.

It turned out that the only asbestos that was found in the building was wrapped around the pipes in the crawl space under the first floor and in the boiler room. The only entrance to the crawl space was through a trap door in the custodian's office. An inspection of the pipes that contained the asbestos found them in good condition. There was no flaking.

The engineers kept me up to date on what was happening with regard to the air quality measurements. I was informed as to what the measurements meant and what the plans were to correct any problem. Whenever I received any information from the experts, I wrote a memo to the staff detailing the findings. I also composed a memo that was given to the students to be brought home. The PTA was kept informed by periodic meetings with the officers. When there was enough information a full PTA evening meeting was scheduled. We were told that asbestos is only dangerous when it is air-bourn and breathed into the lungs. All air quality tests showed the air to be free of asbestos. That information was thoroughly explained to those who attended the meeting.

For the most part parents were concerned but were willing to listen to what was being done. But there were those skeptics that thought we were not telling the whole truth. Proving that you are telling the truth is very difficult. No matter what you say there are those who think you are hiding something from them and the more you say the more they think that. I made a point of saying that in addition to being concerned for the well being of their children, I breathe the same air as their children. Why would I be lying?

One woman came up to see me after the meeting ended. She was visibly angry and was still convinced that I was not telling the whole truth. The interesting thing was that she had a cigarette in her hand. In the 1970s though smoking was known to be harmful, it was not yet banned from public places as it is today. I asked this woman if she smoked at home and around her children. She admitted that she did. Being an x-smoker I seized upon the opportunity to tell her how much more dangerous her smoking was to her child than the contained asbestos we had in the school.

The lesson learned was that it was easier for this woman to blame others than to hold herself responsible for her own bad behavior. Perception is often more believable than fact!

Calculators in Kindergarten? Change Comes Hard

Change frightens some people and especially if it is directed at their young children.

I was observing an arithmetic lesson being given by Mrs. Ryan in her Kindergarten class. I must admit that I was not used to seeing arithmetic being taught at the Kindergarten level, but there it was.

The children were counting various objects in the classroom. They then put their chairs into groups of four and counted the number of groups. They used all kinds of props for their counting and groupings. I was very impressed.

I told Mrs. Ryan in our post-observation discussion how impressed I was with her planning and teaching. One thing led to another when she said that the only thing holding these students back from delving further into arithmetic was their lack of knowledge of the multiplication tables. "That's not a problem" I said, "They could use calculators." Simple calculators were very cheap then and I told her that I could buy one for each student if she felt she could teach the children how to use them. She loved the idea and so did I. The other two Kindergarten teachers said they would like to try it too. Good deal! Every Kindergartener would be taught to use a calculator.

I bought the calculators and gave them to the teachers. Within a week, Mrs. Ryan invited me back to observe an arithmetic lesson using the new calculators. Wow is all I could say. The students counted one row and one column of floor tiles and, using their calculators, told how many tiles there were in the room. They then counted each tile individually and of course got the same answer as they got using multiplication with their calculators. Kindergartners were able to understand what multiplication did and how to use the knowledge. The kids, the teacher and I were very pleased.

That months PTA meeting was very well attended. In fact there were far more parents there than I expected. The reason soon became apparent to me. There were a number of Kindergarten parents in the audience. It also became apparent that they were there to question the use of calculators in their child's Kindergarten class.

I explained how the lesson I observed both before and after the use of calculators had impressed me and why we decided to use them. Most parents nodded in agreement but some expressed their concerns. They said their children would not learn their multiplication tables if they used calculators. I agreed and explained that the plan was to introduce the tables in later grades without using calculators. In the meantime, these 5 year olds were learning concepts and using a tool for solving problems.

There were some parents who agreed, some that were wait and see and some that kept up the questioning saying, "What if the battery had gone dead", or "The kids didn't have their calculator with them? How could they do the math?" At this point, a thought popped into my head that I meant to be funny as well as informative. I said, "Using the same logic then we should be teaching the kids how to use smoke signals in case their telephone was not working." That went over like a lead balloon.

I must admit I thought it was funny when I said it as did some people but not everyone agreed. I don't advise using that kind of humor to advocate for any change especially for 5 year olds. I should have included the Kindergarten parents in the process long before the PTA meeting.

But let me make one thing clear. I believe change is important and more important today than ever before. Too often people think that the way they were taught was the right way and the only way to teach. Just think, these people were in Kindergarten more than twenty-five years ago. The knowledge needed today is so different than it was then. New tools for teaching and learning are being developed at lightning speed. Curriculums should be changing to accommodate new material. Educators must prepare students for the world in which they will live. To deny them that is to leave them in the dust! We don't know what the world will look like in twenty years. So how about teaching how to learn!

Learning needs change in order to never go out of style.

Chapter 3

Learning and Teaching

Whether as a teacher, principal or central administrator, I always thought of myself as a Teacher. Just as that master teacher shared her knowledge and methods with me when I started, I have shared mine with those whom I have supervised. Following is a plan for a lesson that I have shared with others and used myself.

Anatomy Of A Lesson - Getting ready to learn.

Classroom management: Take care of anything that might interrupt the lesson such as bathroom visits, drinks and sharpening pencils. Have the students clear their desks except for what is needed. I would say, "Put on your thinking cap." I had a hat that I would put on to signal the new mode.

Set the objective: What will they learn about in this lesson? Prepare them for the things they will be doing such as viewing a film, or listening to a tape.

Motivation: Why should they know this? How will they use it? Will this be fun to learn? How can I make it interesting? How can I get the class to think, "Need to Know"?

Pre-assessment: What do the students already know? Build from that.

How is this lesson relative: Does what they already know relate to what the lesson is going to be about?

Teacher presentation: List, pronounce, spell and define any words that will be used in the lesson.

Relate examples to past experiences: Point to and emphasize the new vocabulary as it is presented during the lesson. Use the new vocabulary often.

Periodic Checking: Take the time to determine that understanding is taking place before you go on. If you find the lesson is not understood by many students use a different way to explain it.

Don't Just Say It! Model It: Show the students how you do it. Explain your thought processes by thinking aloud as you perform the task.

Change Modes: Cater to different learning styles by changing modes of delivery during the lesson. Seeing, hearing, doing, touching and discussing are all modes to be considered.

Questioning Techniques: Set rules for answering questions. If you say "raise your hand and wait until I call on you," stick to it! The student whose hand is raised waiting to be called on learns a bad lesson when the teacher allows a call-out response.

Try having students stand up instead of raising their hand. That will get their blood moving. Leave enough time for those who need it, to think a little longer before you call on someone. Use whole class "call-out answers" when appropriate. "On a count of three, class, call out your answer. 1, 2, 3, go!"

Be sensitive to the learner's ego when a wrong answer is given.

Remember anything that may be considered ridicule will chill not only the one who answered incorrectly but many others as well. However, don't be so sensitive that you allow a wrong answer to go uncorrected.

There are no "dumb" questions or answers. Most students would rather be considered "bad" or "lazy" than "dumb". So, they may be misbehaving in order to cover up their difficulties with learning. Keep questions and answers on the topic. Like the Internet, it is very easy to go off on a tangent that leads you away from your objective. Use your "back" button!

Independent activity: After the whole class lesson, sum up what has been learned and plan an independent activity to reinforce the skills that were taught.

Homework: For practice or for fun, but not for new learning! Practice doesn't make perfect, perfect practice makes perfect!

Assessment: Paper and pencil, questions and answers or demonstration can all be used to determine how much they learned and what needs to be reviewed. Use them all.

Review & Reinforce: Take a few minutes

Remember, memory is enhanced with periodic tweaking!

Put On a Play

My first full time class was a fourth grade in an all white, middle class, upward mobile Long Island community. I was very excited about my new assignment and couldn't wait to get started. After the first month, I wondered if I had chosen the wrong profession. I was so tired at the end of each day that I was barely able to mark papers and read a newspaper before going to sleep. I caught every cold that the children were more than willing to give me and my once powerful voice was down to a whisper due to my recurring case of laryngitis.

I was sitting in the lunchroom relaxing and happy for a little peace and quiet when a fellow fourth grade teacher asked me how I was doing. Of course, I said, "Great" but she read my response differently. She told me how the first year is the hardest and that I was probably making all the mistakes a new teacher makes like wanting the kids to like me instead of respect me. She was right. I complained that I had a class full of bickering ten year olds. They fought with each other and didn't show much respect for their fellow classmates. They loved it when we were fooling around but when it was time to get serious I had to raise my voice to get their attention.

"Put on a play." What? She repeated, "Put on a play. That's the best way to get the class to work together." She went on to explain how putting on a play contains all the training needed by the class and me. I was willing to try it and she said she would help.

Her advice: First, look for a play that has many short, speaking parts. Choose one that needs costumes and scenery and above all, one that is at the interest level of their age group. Then devote most of the next three weeks of class time to preparing for the performance date.

I announced the plan to the class and it got their attention. I chose six short stories taken from Aesop's Fables and read them to the class. The students were to discuss ideas for each one and vote on the three they would like to produce. Each story had a wonderful moral lesson that the students could relate to. They each had interesting costumes and scenery that the art teacher and parents could get involved with. We were on our way.

Being the producer of this play was a most exciting project. I was as busy as I had ever been but the time spent was most rewarding for both the students and me. The kids worked together helping each other memorize lines. They painted scenery and designed costumes with the help of their parents and our wonderful art teacher. Above all, they were all working together to reach our mutual goal.

Our first rehearsal showed us what had to be done to get ready for what I called "The Moment Of Truth" that moment when the curtain opens and the audience waits to see the performance. I used that phrase on numerous occasions to refocus their attention to the task. We worked on voice projection, eye contact and timing. I spoke about how important each person's part was in making the finished product. Above all, I watched the class come together in their common cause.

Three performances were planned one for each half of the student body of the school and an evening performance for parents, grandparents and other relatives. The "Moment Of Truth" came each time the curtains parted and the kids saw the audience staring at them in anticipation. It is that moment when a hush comes over the audience and all eyes are looking at you waiting to hear what you are about to say and do. It is truly a unique and memorable experience.

At the end, they all looked at each other with a new respect. They did it! They set out to accomplish a task and they did it! They were all very proud of each other and themselves. The praises coming from other teachers, students and relatives lit up their faces and probably mine too.

The lessons learned from this endeavor are too many to enumerate. I know it made a lasting impression on many of the kids. From time to time, even years later, kids who played a part in the production reminded me of "The time we put on a play."

I went on to make many mistakes that first year but I considered the year a success mainly due to putting on that play. Thank you my mentor!

The Best Teaching I Ever Did

I was asked to teach a six weeks summer school for the top 24 fifth and sixth graders in the district. Each of the six elementary schools chose their best two fifth graders and two sixth graders. I had long been an advocate for challenging the top students who I felt were short changed in our effort to help only those who were failing. This was the chance I was looking for. This would show that bright students need attention in reaching their potential every bit as much as those who needed extra help for passing tests.

I would have the attention of these 24 top students for 6 weeks during the summer. The buildings were not air-conditioned and there were certainly many things that these youngsters could do with their time off from school so I felt the challenge to make these 30 mornings memorable.

The plan was to give them a taste of topics that would whet their appetite for science and math.

Week 1 Photography:

Photography would be a good topic to begin with. My good friend and college roommate Frank Manzi was the district's Audio/Visual Director and a natural from whom to get input. The plan was to talk briefly about the history of photography and then get right into it. They would learn the skills for how to make a photographic record of the next 5 weeks.

Day 1: We wasted little time on introductions figuring they would have plenty of time getting to know each other during their cooperative learning experiences. Frank and I motivated them regarding photography and distributed the shoeboxes that they would use to make their own pinhole camera. We talked about exposure to light and focus. They divided into teams of two to help each other with the placement and size of the pinhole. We demonstrated how a pinhole camera would work. Then we set the teams to work on their own pinhole camera. The 4 hours flew by.

Day 2: We talked about composition and how important it was to hold the camera still. We talked about the properties of light. We talked about what to expect in the "Dark Room". Then we went to the high school photo lab. Twenty-four students and two teachers would make it a little tight so we talked about claustrophobia. Using only a red safe light Frank and I demonstrated how to load the light sensitive photo paper into the back of their pinhole camera and seal it up so that it would be light tight. Then it was their turn. That ended day two.

Day 3: In addition to their pinhole camera, each team was given a disposable thirty-five millimeter camera. Their assignment was for each team to tell a five-picture story using their disposable camera and for each student to take one shot with their pinhole camera.

Day 4: Back to the lab. We reviewed exposure time and talked about the chemical process and function of the "developer", "short stop" and "hypo". We spoke about how critical the temperature of the chemicals could be. Then for the magic! Frank and I developed our pinhole photos. If you have ever experienced the magic of seeing the image appear from the blank paper in the developer you will understand the thrill each student felt as they developed the results of their pinhole camera.

Day 5: using construction paper, the teams helped each other make and decorate frames for their pinhole photos. They were to use the remaining film in their disposable cameras to photograph the activities of the next five weeks. They talked to each other about their experiences of the past four days. I sat back and let them talk. The last part of the day was spent starting a journal that they would keep for the rest of the classes.

Week 2 Astronomy:

Day 1: We brainstormed about the sun, the stars, the moon, the planets, distances and other thoughts generated during our discussion. The planets captured most of their interest. Teams were formed to research information about the sun and the planets of our solar system. I ended the session with telling them that we would be going by bus to the local planetarium for day two. We were all excited about our next adventure.

Day 2: We boarded a bus and were off to the planetarium with our cameras and notebooks. The show focused on the planets that circle the sun of our solar system. Perfect! On the ride back, I told the very excited group that astronomy was best taught at night and not in a classroom but outside using telescopes. So day 3 would be held in the field behind the school and begin at 8:00 PM. Their parents were invited to join the class.

Day 3: The local astronomy club had been contacted and eight people came to the schoolyard with their telescopes. They were happy to show off their knowledge and we were thrilled to have them do so. They set up their telescopes to follow the moon and whatever planets were visible for that night. We were very lucky! The moon was just a sliver so its light did not overpower the sky. Jupiter, Mars and Saturn were in view for that night. How fortunate was that?

When parents came to pick up their child they asked if they could see what the telescopes were looking at. You can imagine their excitement. At almost midnight, I finally got the parents and kids to go home, but they agreed only after I promised to have another night session on the next day.

Day 4. As promised, the class met at 8:00 PM. This time we had ten people with telescopes ready to show us the night sky. We also had all the parents stay for the show. I could not have been happier with the night's activity. The kids were eager to tell the parents what they had already learned and the parents were beaming about what they saw. For me this was the most rewarding teaching I had ever done.

Day 5. We were back in the classroom exchanging comments made by their parents. They were so proud! The final half hour was dedicated to writing in their journals.

Week 3 Biology & Health:

We chose the unit on Biology because some special activities were available to us. First, we had access to the Biology Lab at the high school. Some students who were planning to become teachers offered to help us with slides and microscopes. They showed our students what Paramecium and other microbes looked like under high power.

The highlight of the unit was a visit to the home of Larry Tooker. Larry was a principal in the district who had a home on a small island located on The Great South Bay. It was a beautiful summer's day when we crossed the small waterway in rowboats to get to his house. Larry conducted a class on the ecology of the island that was wonderful. He loved his audience and the kids loved him.

 The most interesting thing about the lesson was that all five senses were involved in the process. The use of our sense of sight and hearing are obvious. The sense of smell came from the salt air that wafted around us. We dug for clams using our bare feet for locators. That gave us the use of our sense of touch and best of all, by eating the raw clams we utilized our sense of taste. Not everyone liked this last one but how many times has a lesson contained the five senses?

Week 4 Dinosaurs: Museum Of Natural History

Motivation for this unit was a trip to the Museum of Natural History in New York City. Each student had their disposable camera and were taught the three 10s. They were to photograph things of interest from a distance of ten yards, ten feet and ten inches.

The class was divided into groups of four students who were given the freedom to explore their particular interest. The assignment was for each group to report their findings to the rest of the class during the next 4 days. Their imagination and the skills they learned were to be included in order to make their presentation easy to understand and fun to listen to by the rest of the class.

Days two and three were to be used for gathering information and preparing their presentations. We talked about the skills associated with speaking to groups including things like eye contact and voice modulation. Just as important as the presenters were the listeners. They were taught to be good listeners and ask relevant questions.

Days four and five were to be used for presenting, listening and of course writing in their journals.

Week 5 Biography:

For this unit we divided the group into teams of two. One would take on the persona of a famous person and the other would interview that person. Then they would switch roles. They were to present their information without giving out the name of the person they were portraying until they were finished or when someone correctly called out the name.

On day one, they split into teams and chose the person they would portray. The rest of days one, two and three were spent gathering information and preparing their presentations. We spoke about using their imagination to make their presentations interesting as well as challenging for the rest of the class.

Day four and five were presentation days. Some came in costumes they had made at home. Without going into detail suffice it to say, there were some wonderful presentations that filled the rest of the week. Their assignment was to get their throwaway camera film developed in time for week 6.

Week 6 Communication & Culmination:

The final week was dedicated to reviewing the previous five weeks. They were to use their journal entries as well as their photographs to write a composition describing their impressions of the preceding five weeks. I would collect them and add comments. They would then put it into final copy condition to be kept as a memento.

We invited their parents to the final day's session to listen to these comments. Each student read his or her comments to the applause of both parents and fellow classmates. The accolades from parents were spilling over. I felt like a million bucks.

The next year the budget was defeated and the summer program was discontinued!

Disappointment sometimes comes with the territory.

Chapter 4

Keep Away From Downers
Flickism

I learned this lesson while serving in the United States Army.

I was drafted on December 7th, twelve years after Pearl Harbor. After some harrowing days of getting ready, I began my basic training. It was scheduled for eight weeks during which time we were to learn how to take orders, go on long marches, fire weapons, eat army chow in a huge mess hall and be subjected to Kitchen Patrol (KP) to name a few new experiences. Those 8 weeks in Fort Dix were the coldest I have ever been in my life.

The main thing for getting through this period was to keep a sense of humor and stay away from those who didn't have one. Most of the guys felt the same way but there was always one who could find something to complain about. Flick was one of those. No matter what the situation was, he would make the worst of it. I kept as far away from him as I could.

The next assignments were posted on the last day of the eight-week cycle. Having been a teacher, I was sure that I would be assigned to some desk job. Not so! There was my name along with the others for another eight weeks of Advanced Infantry Basic. To add insult to injury I was given KP and the worst job of all, cleaning pots and pans on that day. To say the least this was not going to be a good day.

My friend Ed and I had worked for three hours scrubbing pots and pans before it came time to have our breakfast. I was sitting with my friend when who should come walking along holding a tray and looking for a place to sit? Flick! Ed was about to call him over to join us. I begged him not to but he assured me that Flick had changed. With that, Flick saw us and sat down next to me. He was sobbing! Real tears were rolling down his cheeks. He said, "I am going to kill myself!" I think he really meant it. I looked at my friend and without speaking a word, sarcastically nodded to thank him.

When I told the story to the other guys, someone who knew him said, "That's a Flickism." It stuck! From that day to this when I run into a downer I think of Flick and I avoid contact as much as I can.

Throughout my career in education, I met very few Flicks. They were the ones that couldn't wait for three O'clock to "bug out" of school. They knew the number of days to the next holiday or the end of the term. Their retirement day couldn't come soon enough. They seemed to always be in the teacher's room blaming students, parents and the principal for all their problems. I really disliked them. How sad to go through life that way! Fortunately, there were very few of them that I came across in my 43 years.

I found one of these Flicks when I first became the Principal of a new school. When I was a teacher, I would have just kept away from him. However, as the school's Principal it was my duty to see to it that he did the job he was being paid for. I couldn't stop what he was saying in the teacher's room but I could make sure he didn't carry that attitude into the classroom.

I spoke to him about how much better his days would be if he had a more positive attitude. At the same time I carefully checked his plan-book to be sure that it was complete and up-to-date. I observed his lessons and found them to be pretty good. The combination of cajoling and checking started to work. He had a lot of good experience that he could call upon. I praised him whenever I observed a positive behavior. Although he shrugged off the praise knew he liked getting it. Who knows, he may have shed his Flick behavior.

Look for humor to get through the tough times.

Chapter 5

If It "Ain't" Broke...

The Horn Rim

I learned this lesson the hard way, which is often the best way.

The 1955 Chevrolet that I owned at the time had a circular horn rim that allowed me to blow the horn from any position. I began to notice that some areas around the rim were dead. I figured that the rim just needed to be cleaned. I told my wife what I thought had to be done and said I could do it. She said "Take it to a mechanic." I said, "But I think I can do it!" "Take it to a mechanic" she said with more conviction. Her lack of confidence in my ability made me all the more stubborn and adamant about doing it myself.

It was a sunny Sunday and I had finished all my chores. I decided now was the time to fix the car's horn. I got some tools and cleaning material and set to work. The rim was held on with two screws located in the back of the rim. I carefully unscrewed the first screw. It was about two inches long. I then unscrewed the second screw. It came off along with two springs that jumped out at me. After looking on the floor of the car, I found the springs and the rim was free. So far so good! I then carefully cleaned the rim and it's setting.

It was a little difficult getting the springs set and the screws started, but after a few trial and errors, I got them going. I screwed them both down and was ready to see if I had accomplished my task. I tapped the rim and the horn sounded. I continued to tap in different places and the horn sounded. I felt great! With a smile on my face, I invited my wife to hear the results of my work. She was only slightly impressed. I went to sleep that night feeling very good about myself.

At about 3:00 AM it started to rain. The rain got heavier and louder until it came down in torrents. Lightening and thunder accompanied the rain and I was glad to be snuggled down in my bed. Then it happened! The car horn began to blast! I was devastated! I didn't want to go outside in the pouring rain. I wondered how long the battery would last before the blowing horn would stop. My wife tapped me on the shoulder to tell me that my horn was ringing. It became my horn as soon as it started ringing. As if I hadn't heard it. Even in the dark, I could see the expression on her face that said, "Take it to a mechanic."

I was sure the noise was waking the whole neighborhood. I had to do something. I got out of bed, threw on a pair of shoes and trousers and went outside. I was immediately soaked. The noise of the horn was at least 3 times louder outside than inside. The lightening and thunder added to the confusion. What to do? The only thing I could think of was to lift the hood. I found the wires that led to the two horns. I gripped both of them and, with all my might, ripped them out of the horns.

Horror of horrors the noise continued. The horns continued to blow! But how could that be? I was holding the disconnected wires in my hands. With that my neighbor, whose car was on the driveway next to mine, came out of his house. He apologized and said he was having trouble with his horn. It was then that it dawned on me that it was his horn not my horn that was waking the neighborhood.

The next day I took the car to the mechanic to get the wires replaced.

He said, "If It Ain't Broke Don't Fix It."

The Pacing Class:

My predecessor, both as a Principal and Assistant Superintendent, dedicated her life to the education of children. Among other things, she initiated a program called The Pacing Class. The pacing class was a transitional first and second grade class for youngsters who showed maturational lags and learning problems during Kindergarten. The benefits of the class were no more than 14 students to a class, a curriculum designed for their needs and an outstanding teacher. Each elementary school had these classes and each claimed success. The ability to individualize instruction to accommodate each student's needs was the basis for the class.

Youngsters attending first and second grade "Pacing Class" then went on to a regular third grade class. Those two years with a smaller class size and an outstanding teacher seemed to work. Most of these students were ready and did well in the regular third grade and beyond. I am sure the program saved many children from being retained or lost.

One day I visited a first grade pacing class. I noticed that the teacher had a tree cut out of a large piece of poster board. The tree had 12 branches, one for each month of the year. On the branches were leaves containing the names of each of her 14 students. Most of the students were boys and the preponderance of leaves hung from the November branch!

This held true for all the years I visited pacing classes. This just proved that November boys, who give away a year's development to those born a month later, are at a disadvantage right from the start. Let's do the math. The difference of one year translates to 20% of growth and development at that age. During that year skills required for language growth are being formed. Motor skills and eye-hand coordination development are taking place at an accelerated pace. Being 20% behind from the beginning has a great impact on not just learning, but also on how that youngster views himself. If the December boy finds the learning easy and the year younger November boy finds the same learning difficult, what does that do to his feelings of self esteem? This knowledge dictated the advice I gave to people who were going to register their November boys for Kindergarten. My advice was to "Wait until next year." Many heeded the advice and thanked me in later years.

When I became the Assistant Superintendent, I had the opportunity to finally find out if the positive thoughts we held about the pacing program were actually correct. I asked the guidance department of the high school to send me a copy of the records for all the current 10th grade students who had attended a first and second grade pacing class. There were about 70 tenth graders from the six elementary schools attending the high school at that time. I looked at each record and compiled the statistics. I recorded the findings and placed them in a folder called "Pacing Program Worked".

The pacing class students were equal in every way to the students who were not identified as having maturational problems. Some were top, some were middle and some were low. Since these students who were failing in Kindergarten did as well as the students who did not need the program that proved to me that the intervention worked. I shared my findings with all the elementary school principals and they shared it with their teachers.

After two years, I left the position of Assistant Superintendent and became the Principal of another elementary school in the district. The person who followed me came from outside the district. He was not part of the district during the time the Pacing Class Program was planned. In addition, his career was mainly in secondary school education, not at the elementary school level. He initiated many new programs and deleted many that were then being practiced. One of those that he deleted was the Pacing Program.

I told him about the study I had done that would show him that the program was well worth keeping. I asked him to look at the report. I don't know if he did! All the elementary school principals appealed to him to leave the Pacing Program in tact. His reply was that modern theory was opposed to this type of class. We tried to explain that this was a special program that had been successful for all these years. But his mind was made up. That was the end of a good program!

When you have the power, use it seldom.

Chapter 6

Better Bad Than Stupid

Barnaby

I learned this lesson thanks to a very special youngster. I had just moved to a new and very different school district. I moved from a North Shore, white-collar district to a South Shore, blue-collar district.

There were many differences between the two districts but the one that stood out most was the different experiences the students had. The kids from the white-collar area had been exposed to many broadening experiences. Aside from where the Army took me, they had done far more traveling than me. On the other hand, most of the kids from the blue-collar community had never been more than 50 miles from home. Many had not even been to New York City a scant forty miles away.

Another glaring difference was the reaction of the parents regarding their children. The white-collar parents questioned everything I said or did. I enjoyed explaining the reasons to them. When I finished and they agreed with what I said they were very cooperative.

On the other hand, the blue-collar parents were more accepting of whatever I said or did. When I called a parent to discuss an issue I may have been having with their child I usually got unquestioned cooperation. Often I didn't even have to go into great detail about the problem. If the teacher said it, the kid was wrong, period. I much preferred the questioning parents. Then I knew that what I said was understood as well as agreed to.

This difference was also evident in the way the students behaved. The blue-collar kids knew that a call to their parents from the teacher meant punishment at home. In fact, I had to make it very clear to parents when I called to praise their child and that this was a complimentary call.

The behavior of the students in my first class in the new district was quite varied. Most of the 32 students did what they were told without question. One unruly boy named Barnaby made up for all the others by constantly getting into trouble. I had to speak to him about his misbehavior many times during the day.

I looked at his record and spoke to his previous teachers and all agreed that he was a major problem. His best conduct grade was a "D". He was defiant and could only read on a second grade level. His math was surprisingly good but his poor reading skills affected all the other subjects. In spite of that, he was considered to be a leader by his fellow classmates. The other students seemed to fear him and respect him. At first I thought that was due to his being bigger and stronger than the other boys, the result of being retained but that was not the case. Though nobody messed with him, he was not a bully. However, he certainly lived up to his reputation as a problem in the classroom. He seldom did his homework or his class work. I had to discipline him more than any other student.

One day another boy came to class wearing a hat. He was a quiet kid not particularly liked by the others. He looked particularly down as he took his seat and left his hat on. For whatever reason at the time everyone removed their hat when they entered the classroom so he having not, made him standout from the rest. Some of the other boys teased him and one snatched the hat from his head. The reason for his behavior immediately became evident. He was completely bald! In fact his head and eyebrows were completely shaved.

The students in the class were as shocked as I was. Some started laughing and pointing at George. I didn't know quite how to handle the situation when Barnaby put his arm around George and looking at the class said that George had been punished enough and that everyone should leave him alone. His words were heard and respected by all the students in the class and they all complied. There was no more laughter. I didn't have to say a word. Barnaby's words said it all. This was a different Barnaby than his records and behavior would indicate. I decided to take a deeper look at this young man

I gave the class an assignment to get them busy and I called George out into the hall. What he told me shocked me to my core.

George's father owned a Bar and Grill. It seems that George was caught taking money from the register. His punishment was to have all the hair on his head and eyebrows shaved off. This was done to humiliate him when he got back to school and it sure did.

At my first opportunity to talk to Barnaby privately, I took the opportunity to praise him for his behavior with George. He shrugged it off saying that no one deserved to be treated like that. I delved further and found a youngster more sensitive than he ever let on. But why was he, the class discipline problem, the most sensitive and understanding of George's problem?

I made it my business to find time to talk to him alone. There was definitely a nice kid behind the façade he showed in class. The more I probed the closer I came to the motivation for his ill behavior.

His reading problems, then called Dyslexia, caused him an immense amount of humiliation. He was ashamed of his inability to read and do any of the work that required that skill. His retention was devastating to him. All the understanding and remedial help he received only increased his embarrassment. He felt that every fellow student as well as his well meaning-teachers were in fact, mocking him. His defense was to misbehave. He would rather be considered "Bad than Stupid!" These were his words that he told me after we had established a close relationship.

I wish I could end this chapter saying that I cured his learning disability but I can't. I did not have the knowledge or the ability to know why he and I could look at the same set of letters that formed into words for me and formed a jumble of symbols for him. The best I could do was try to tell him it was not his fault and that he had other special talents that he could be proud of. I hope what I tried to convey to Barnaby had as lasting and positive an effect on him as it had on me. I always remember the lesson I learned from him

"I'd rather be considered Bad than Stupid!"

Chapter 7

"Shout It Out" All Together Now

The questioning of students is a very common tool used by teachers. I would ask a question to find out if the students understood what I had just taught. I would tell the class to raise their hand and wait to be called on. Some kids raised their hand and waited to be called on, some just blurted out the answer. I realized that this punished the kids who were following directions while the ones who blurted the answer felt good about showing off what they knew. I decided to become very strict with those who didn't wait to be called on. They were not permitted to answer the next few questions. Most times when I called upon a student and the answer given was correct I assumed that the rest of the class got it. Not necessarily!

I became aware that when I posed a question the same hands would be raised. Some strained to show that they knew the answer and waited for a chance to show it. I would call upon a student who often answered the question correctly. All the hands would go down and many students showed a look of rejection at not having been called on. Sometimes the first person got the answer wrong. That caused an even greater exuberance of hand raising and embarrassment to the person whose answer was incorrect. This was not good!

I decided to take notice of my questioning techniques. The first thing I noticed was that the same kids raised their hands and were the ones I most often called upon. Then I looked at those who had never raised their hand. Why was that? I figured they knew the answer but did not wish to volunteer. Maybe they were just shy. Maybe they didn't want to expose themselves to ridicule! What if they didn't know the answer and needed more explanation? I would never know that by the way I was questioning. How could I do this better?

Very often, the question I posed required a one-word or short phrase answer. When this was the case, I went to the "Shout It Out" method. I would pose the question and give the students a few seconds to get ready with their answer. Then on a count of three they would shout out their answer. The kids loved permission to shout out in class and it gave many more students a chance to show they knew the correct answer. Even those who never volunteered felt comfortable shouting out the answer. In the meantime, I would look to see how many did not shout it out. The response of the class would let me know whether more explanation was needed or I could go on with the lesson.

I always wondered what became of the caller outers when they grew up. Well the other day I found out. They just become adult caller outers! I am the leader of a group of two-dozen men that meet once a month. We discuss current events. We are a very diverse group. In order to keep order I ask members to raise their hand and wait to be called on. One member continually interrupts and calls out. I explained the reason and asked him to raise his hand and wait to be called on. At the next meeting, he raised his hand but also called out. I told him that he was half way there. He had to raise his hand and wait to be called on! I would love to ask him if he used to call out when he was a young student.

If you set rules stick to them.

Chapter 8

Pavlov's Dog

What A Way to Begin

The time was March just two months after I had become the Principal of the brand new John F. Kennedy Elementary School. I had taught at the elementary school level for thirteen years and completed all the academic requirements for becoming a principal. As a teacher, I was often put in charge of the building when, Mr. Ames, the Principal was away. I thought I was ready for this new assignment. I soon realized I had a lot to learn.

As I sat in the office thinking of what I should be doing, I realized that there were parts of the building that I needed to know about. I sought out Pat Caldwell, the very competent head custodian of the building. He knew the building from top to bottom and was very proud to have been chosen to take care of it.

I asked him to escort me on a tour of the building and fill me in on what I should know. One of the first places we stopped at was the fire alarm system. Pat showed me how to set and unset the alarm. He told me that everyone had to exit the building in less than two minutes. I asked him how many more practice drills we had to have. Ten drills were required for the year and there were four left to do. Satisfied that I knew what I needed to know, I returned to my office and scheduled the four required drills for later in the year.

As I was sitting at my desk not more than a few days after my tour with the head custodian, I heard the blaring sound of the three loud bells that signaled an alarm. WHAT IS THAT? I quickly looked out the window to confirm that it was a miserable winter's day on Long Island. Freezing rain was pelting against the windows. What was Pat thinking? Setting a fire drill in this weather? I rushed out and headed for his office with anger in my eyes. I couldn't believe that he could have done such a thing without even consulting me first.

He came out of his office with the same look in his eyes. He couldn't believe that this new principal who was still wet behind the ears could do this. When we looked at each other we both realized that this was not a drill. Neither of us pulled the alarm. There could be a fire!

The teachers and students were already leaving the building as they were conditioned to do. I stood by one of the exit doors watching the looks on the glaring eyes of the teachers as they passed out of the building. They left without even their coats on for protection against the elements. In less than two minutes, the only people left in the building were Ben and I. I ran to the second floor, Pat covered the first floor as we both looked for the reason the alarm was sounded. Neither of us found any smoke or other dangerous problems. We looked at each other and decided to press the all-clear signal and the school filled again. This time it filled with a shivering, wet and rather confused group of teachers, students and other personnel.

Pat and I agreed that we would call the manufacturers and installers of the system and have them come to the school that afternoon. We called the Superintendent and told him what had happened and what we planned to do. He agreed and said he would make some calls and to keep him posted.

I returned to my office to wait for the dismissal of the students so we could start the investigation. It was no more than an hour later that the alarm went off again! Pat and I knew this was the result of something wrong with the system but like Pavlov's Dog, the children and teachers were well trained and left the building. This time they had no doubt that this was the doing of their new Principal who was showing off his new power.

As the last person left the building I quickly rang the all-clear signal and watched the school refill again. I figured two months on the job and this was what the kids were going home to tell their parents about school that day. Great!

Finally, the buses came and the children were on their way home. The teachers were close behind them anxious to get into warm, dry clothing. The thought entered my mind to call a quick meeting so that I could explain that I had nothing to do with the mishap but I thought better of it. They would find out sooner-or-later. Within minutes of the children's arrival home, the phones began to ring. With some variations, they all asked why I had called a fire drill in this weather. My two secretaries were busy explaining to irate parents that this was not a called for drill. It signaled a problem.

That afternoon the installers came to the school and were almost as anxious as Pat and I to find out what set off the alarm. The volunteer fire department was also came. Every smoke and fire detector was checked and rechecked. They were fine! They checked and rechecked the wiring for a faulty connection.

We spent the next several hours trying to solve the mystery but no explanation was found. Every time the installers were about to give up I would simply say, "Something set the alarm off and there is no reason to believe that it will not happen again. Please keep looking!"

Finally they said they had tightened every fitting and checked every detector and there was nothing more they could do at this time short of disabling the entire system. That was not an option. They promised to work on the problem back at the plant. They reset the system saying the building had to be protected. With that, they packed up and left. Pat and I looked at each other and were not convinced but we could do no more.

Months went by and just as people seemed to forget the incident suddenly and without warning, three loud bells indicating an alarm sounded. Fortunately it was a warm, sunny, Spring Day and we needed another drill to fill our required number for the year. Like Pavlov's experiment proved, everyone left the building in an orderly manner and returned after the all-clear bell sounded.

Afterward Pat and I met in the hall each looking puzzled and concerned. We began the process again that had not found the reason for the two mishaps on that fateful winter's day. Once again, we found nothing. But we informed the Superintendent and the alarm company of the event.

As I waited for dismissal and another try at finding the cause a boy came to my office. He was a bit frightened and told me that he thought he had set off the alarm. Elated I jumped up and told him he was not in trouble but to please show me how he thinks he did it. I called Pat and we followed the boy to the staircase at the end of the hall. Half way up the stairs the boy explained that he tossed a newspaper up in the air and it hit the smoke alarm. In a second or two the alarm went off. I was ready to hug the kid but thanked him and sent him back to class.

When school was done, Pat got a ladder and looked into the smoke alarm. There, very contented looking, sat a large spider. Ben explained that the smoke detector worked as follows. A beam of light is aimed at a mirror that reflects the light back to a light meter. The smoke alarm was set to sound the alarm whenever the light that bounced off the mirror was interrupted by smoke. Apparently, the spider somehow did exactly that three times. Pat and I looked at each other and smiled. That problem was solved!

The result was that the manufacturer placed a screen around all the smoke detectors they had installed so that no spider could enter and set off the alarm again.

This was one more situation that was not taught at Graduate School.

Chapter 9

Integrated Learning/Teaching

Learning From a Master Teacher

During my first year as a fourth grade teacher, I was fortunate to have taught next door to a master teacher. I was going page by page through the textbooks using my personality to keep interest high for my students. Next door to my classroom was a master teacher who had the students doing all kinds of interesting projects. There was a constant buzz of activity going on. Kids worked together or were writing in journals or doing artwork. The music and art teachers were involved. The kids looked very busy and well into their lessons. It looked great! But was it all just fun and were they learning what was supposed to be learned for the grade? As it turned out her students did better than mine on every test. I asked her to teach me how she did it.

First off, she said that I was to do my first year by the book in order to learn the curriculum. After becoming familiar with the curriculum for the grade, I could get into a Thematic Teaching Unit. "But" she said "Since you are so interested in learning the method, I will help you through one now."

She proceeded to tell me how an integrated unit works and helped me through the first one. After that, I was hooked. It was not only fun for the students but I enjoyed teaching that way. Some years ago I decided to write the method down so that I could pass it on to teachers who were interested. It follows:

Thematic Teaching:

A thematic teaching unit is a method of teaching the subject matter that is contained in the curriculum using a central theme that incorporates the various disciplines. In addition to learning the facts and skills for each subject, students learn to organize their thinking, work cooperatively with others, locate information that is pertinent to their assignment and   prepare to deliver both a written and an oral presentation. They were to present it to their peers and parents, which would get them the satisfaction that only comes with producing something worthwhile.

Why Use A Thematic Unit?

Unlike the traditional way of presenting specific bits of knowledge that are to be memorized, a thematic unit cuts across subjects to form a whole picture. The process of writing, speaking and presenting what they have learned creates a "Gestalt" where the whole is greater than the sum of its parts. Instead of listening to and then regurgitating what was memorized, students become active learners. They learn how to learn! Memorization of facts is highly rewarding for the system of assessment in schools, but of little value in today's "real life".

Need to Know:

There is no greater motivation for learning than the "Need To Know"! I learned this lesson when I was in the Army stationed in Germany back in the '50s. I was attached to a heavy mortar company that spent too much of its time on maneuvers in the woods. Our helmet was filled with cold water in the morning and was to be used for washing my face, brushing my teeth and shaving. I never did figure out the best sequence. This was not the best place for a boy born in Brooklyn to remain.

One day a request for a photographer was posted on the bulletin board. As soon as I read it, I applied. Anything was better than living in a tent or worse in a foxhole. The only problem was that I had little knowledge about photography. I figured I could fake it. I could watch the other guy and follow his lead… no problem!

I met with the lone regimental photographer, Ray Watson and we took an immediate liking for each other. He was being sent back to the states in ten days so that all he spoke about was his home and girl friend in Pennsylvania. He recommended me to the Captain and I got the job.

Now I had to pick Ray's brain about the job! "You need to take photos with a 4x5 Speed Graphic Press camera, develop the negatives and print them in the darkroom. Then you have to send the prints to the 3 newspapers, The 9th Division News, the Army Times and the Stars and Stripes."

Oops! Could I learn this in ten days? To make matters worse, Ray's body was in Germany but his head was in Pennsylvania. I could get only a few answers from him before his eyes would glaze over and he would speak of home. Too soon, the day came when Ray left for home.

I got as much from Ray as I could but it was off to the library to learn what I NEEDED TO KNOW. My motivation was enormous! It was learn and perform or be returned to an angry mortar company commander. The good news was that I had plenty of film and photographic paper to experiment with and Ray had set up a very efficient photo lab.

To make a long story short, I learned in three weeks what would have taken three semesters to teach. I learned by trial and error and getting information from the library but mostly because I NEEDED TO KNOW! The lessons I learned from that experience remained with me and shaped my beliefs for how I would teach.

Teachers can't always provide motivation that is that intense for their students but principals can help them create a need to know learning environment. Instead of going page by page through a textbook and separate subject areas, suggest ways for them to create a "Need to Know" project. Knowing the curriculum, a teacher can integrate teaching the skills from the various subjects and how they relate to each other. For example, the time to teach writing a friendly letter is when the project calls for writing a real friendly letter that relates to the project.

Getting Started:

Select a topic. Topic selection is the very important first step to a successful unit. Look for a topic that fits with your curriculum so that the time spent meets much of the curriculum you are responsible to cover during the year.

Your Social Studies or Science curriculum would be a good place to look. Look to see if something important is going on in the world that is related to the topic. Think through the topic and see how parts of the curriculum could be woven through the unit. For example, if you are responsible for teaching the United States Government, start an electoral unit at the end of September. You are sure to get current news coverage that will reinforce what you are teaching and increase interest in the topic for the upcoming November election. Plus parents will be very impressed when their child can talk to them with some knowledge about the current event.

Be sure that your topic has a good deal of information that is readily available. Your public and school library, textbooks, the media and especially the Internet with a good search engine are great places to begin.

Think about how other subject areas can fit with the topic. For example, if you are doing an election unit, lettering and poster making could be included in the art teacher's lessons. The music teacher could help with campaign jingles for a mock election. Math could be included with predicting outcomes and counting votes. Think fractions and percentages. Get information from newspapers. Your own and your students imagination will be your best tools for this task.

Example of three types of Integrated Units:

Solving a Problem: Teenage smoking or violence in schools.

Making a Choice: A health unit on choosing a favorite cereal.

Becoming an Expert: Biography or How Things Work.

Motivation:

Motivation is the next item. Current events create their own motivation. If your topic is discussed in the media it makes your job that much easier. An Olympics unit will give you two weeks of very exciting coverage. This can be great for learning about countries, where they are, what language they speak, their government and so on.

Some things to consider: a class trip, a film, a guest speaker, a parent who knows the subject or just a lively discussion about how much fun it would be to learn about … you fill in the blank. Your enthusiasm for the topic will rub off on the students. Drop some hints about the interesting things that they will learn from doing this unit. Help students realize that they will be using their own imagination and skills to produce their exhibit or presentation.

Develop the outline: In a whole group discussion, list items that would relate to the topic. Write every suggestion given by the students on a chart. When suggestions slow down, you can begin the process of narrowing down. Combine similar entries. Modify items that are slightly off the topic. Suggest that items that are way off the topic may be used in a different unit. The remaining items will form the basis for the individual or group assignment.

Group Rules: Cooperative learning skills are an often-neglected part of the learning process. Thematic teaching fosters learning and using these skills. In a whole class discussion, list those items that would go into making for good cooperation and teamwork. This might be a good place for the Physical Education teacher to reinforce the concept of teamwork in his or her class. List those things that are helpful and those that are hurtful. A set of rules should come out of the discussions and be agreed upon by the class. Each student will be provided a written copy of the rules that they sign onto.

Group Selection: Groups consisting of two to four students are the most efficient. There are numerous ways to make up the groups. Sometimes, I did a sociogram with the class to determine the leaders and followers and used that information to make up the teams. I would have each student write the names of three students who they thought they would like to work with. If the numbers show a good spread then your job is easy and each student can have their first choice. If not you will have to look at their second and third choices. Make sure that each group has a good mix of abilities. Some negotiating may be necessary to accomplish this task. Then you make up the groups. Letting the students choose for themselves often leads to hard feelings and some unhappy kids.

Group Cohesion: Allow time for the groups to get together to talk about their skills, interests and abilities. They should get to know each other and appreciate each-others individuality. Have each one list what they can bring to this assignment and share it with their group.

Group Assignments: With a four-person team you might have the following assignments: Facilitator, Recorder, Researcher and

Presenter. These assignments are fluid. All members will at some time assume the roll for each of these positions. It is important that everyone know the function for every assignment so that when it is their turn, they will know what to do. Every member has responsibility for the success of the other team member's assignment.

The Facilitator: keeps the team focused on the task, sets the time, place and agenda for team meetings and checks to see that the assignments are completed.

The Recorder: takes notes of the meeting and gathers any information provided by the team.

The Researcher: looks for information related to the topic for distribution to the team.

The Presenter: plans for the presentation.

The Research Cycle: The research cycle should be taught after the topic has been selected and before work on the project begins. I'll use a unit on Cereal as an example.

The Project's Goal: To gather information that relates to health, cost and taste of the cereals investigated and to share that information with others in an interesting and creative presentation.

Questioning: The questions raised during the brainstorming session will give direction to the unit.

What are the ingredients in cereal?

Where in the world do they come from?

How much do they cost per ounce... per pound?

Which one tastes the best?

Which are the healthiest?

What makes a cereal healthy?

Which box design catches your eye?

Planning: Using these questions, the team develops strategies for finding the information. A log should be kept listing the resources used, by whom, when and where.

A. Go to a supermarket and look at the ingredients on the cereal boxes.

B. Search the ingredients on the Internet.

C. Compare total price and price per ounce.

D. Do a blindfold taste test.

E. Check for sugar and fat content.

F. Poll the rest of the school for their favorite cereal.

Gathering: Information is gathered and saved for easy access. This would be the time for a class lesson on note taking and advancing skills in doing Internet searches. Do a search for the enormous amount of material from websites like Kellogg, the American Heart Association and Weight Watchers to name a few. This would be a good time to present a how-to lesson for ways to write emails to these companies.

Sorting: Sort the information into sub-topics. Placing the information on 3x5 cards will make the task easier.

This would be a good time to teach an arithmetic lesson from the information that is listed on the box. Make a template that has the information you want from each company. Include things like: the name – the number of ounces in the box – the total price – the price per ounce- the serving size – calories per serving - % of calories from fat and so on.

The list of ingredients and where in the world they come from could be the motivation for a Social Studies lesson.

Synthesizing: The pertinent information is then integrated and made ready for evaluation. Ask the question, "How does this piece of information fit with the project's goals?"

A. Economic reasons

B. Taste reasons

C. Nutritious reasons

Evaluating: During the evaluation the team may decide to repeat any or all of the previous steps in order to refine the information and prepare for the presentation.

The Presentation: How will the team present their project to the rest of the class and you? Here is where each team member's imagination will be tested. Every member must be involved in both the written and oral portion of the presentation. They must present their part and explain all the steps taken to arrive at their conclusions. They can use visuals, audio or anything else they can think of to advance their point of view.

Plan a whole class lesson on the skills needed for public speaking. Search the Internet using the key phrase "Public Speaking" for information. The speech teacher might be a good resource to tap or how about the principal?

Plan a lesson about what it takes to be a good audience.

Invite parents, other teachers and the principal to the presentation.

Point out the many skills that were learned in order to get the students to complete their tasks.

Show how the New York State Standards were incorporated in the lessons.

Assessment: The final step in the process is assessment. It should start with a whole class discussion that lists the skills and knowledge for which they will be graded. This must take place at an early stage of the project and be reinforced periodically.

Some of the skills are:

A. How well did each student work within the team?

B. How did each student find and contribute their information?

C. How organized was the student and the team?

D. How well prepared was the team for its presentation?

E. What skills were taught and how well were they learned?

F. Have each student do a self-evaluation and one for the team.

G. Have each team select one thing they could have done better.

The skills learned along the way in a thematic unit often become a lifelong learning experience. It gives students a chance to express their sense of humor and creativity while learning the subject matter.

In all my years, I have found no better way to teach or learn.

Chapter 10

Raising Expectations

The "Good Scholarship Association":

A Lobby for Learning

It dawned on me one day that various parent groups were very successful in getting support from the Board of Education for their pet projects. The Football Parents Association got goodies paid for with district money. The Band Parents got money for instruments and new uniforms so that they could look great when they strutted around the football field. These parents were lobbyists that attended B.O.E. meetings and got the board members to vote for things they needed. Where were the parents of the top students to lobby for "good-scholarship" money? Not!

That was the impetus for some teachers and me starting The Good Scholarship Association (GSA). We got a small group of parents and teachers to form a committee whose main interest was scholarship. The thought was to lobby for those things that advanced learning and scholarship. We brought the idea to the Superintendent. He liked the concept and we went forward with it.

We scheduled a meeting inviting those people who were interested in advocating for good scholarship for the top students from all the grades. Invitations went to teachers, parents and high school students. We geared our meetings to providing information and support for parents and students for how the district could enhance "Good Scholarship".

We devoted the topic for our first GSA meeting to study habits. Notices were sent out to every parent and surprise, surprise we had a great turnout. Our speaker talked about providing a study environment that was conducive to learning. For some it was a very quiet room. For others soft music was best. Parents were given ideas regarding the place, time and environment that was best for their child's study habits. The question and answer period brought out many problems and solutions. We considered it a very successful start.

For our second GSA meeting we invited a financial advisor to tell the parents of elementary school aged students the best way to start saving for college. This brought out even more people and the comments were again very helpful. The speaker told me that he was very impressed with the questions and the comments of the parents.

At another meeting high school parents were invited to hear about college grants and scholarships that were available that very often went begging because not enough people applied for them. They gave the parents and high school students, tips on how to apply for these monies and what to write on their application.

Volunteers offered after school and Saturday tutorial services to students to prepare them for taking the SATs. A "Hot Line" was started to answer questions for students.

Each meeting brought more people and the reputation of the GSA grew into one of the best lobbies that advocated for scholarship. That led to the best idea of all...

College Visitation Day:

Many realize that the decision to attend college has to be made long before the application stage. By the time a student is in high school their plan to attend or not to attend college is pretty well set. So... we set out to introduce the idea in ten-year old minds that college could be a natural progression after high school. In order to "raise their expectations" we set up a "College Visitation Day" not for high school seniors but for all the 5th grade students in the district. We selected fifth graders because we felt that was when children could best be influenced to make positive decisions about going on to college.

We were in touch with local colleges asking them to host a group of 40 or so 5th grade students. We explained that the benefit for their institution was that these students would remember their experiences and become their students of the future. After many phone calls and some cajoling, seven local colleges offered to host a group.

The day came. Buses brought our students to their designated college. I was with the group that went to Farmingdale College. College students who were planning to become teachers met us as we arrived. We divided into smaller groups. Our guide introduced himself and showed us around the campus. He spoke to the kids about college life and how special it was. The best occurred when a group was shown a typical bedroom in the dorm and asked if there were any questions. One student noticed a TV in the room and asked, "Can you watch anything you want?"

We ate lunch in the Student Union with the other college students. Our students wrote about and shared their experiences of that day with their fellow classmates. All the objectives for the day were met. It was a great and memorable day!

After retiring, I went to work at Eastern Suffolk BOCES. One of my assignments was to be a mentor for Frank Garcia, a bi-lingual principal. He turned out to be one of the best principals I have ever known. We hit it off immediately. He was recently reassigned to the school in the district that had all the 3rd, 4th and 5th grade students. The grades were new to him. He asked for a BOCES mentor to help him get started. That's how we met.

A key goal of his was to raise expectations for the students in his charge. The "Dropout Rate" for the students of this district was high and only a very small percentage completed high school and went on to college. I told him about the college visitation day I had done with my home district and he loved the idea. Permission was asked for and granted for the plan by the Superintendent and we got to work.

We selected local colleges that were to be called in order to garner an invitation to visit their school. Those that offered education programs were the first to be called. Some colleges balked at first but agreed after they were told how successful previous experiences had been. The result was that six local colleges agreed to host a morning visitation by our fifth graders.

The six, fifth grade teachers met and selected the college that their class would attend. They discussed ways to build excitement for the students. Art teachers helped with school banners. Music teachers helped students make up cheers for the college they were going to visit. Students surfed the Internet to search for information about "their college". Questions were prepared related to the college. Parents of the students were informed of the plans and were urged to add to the excitement.

Visitation Day finely came. Six busses arrived to transport the kids and teachers to their designated school. Armed with their journal, lunch boxes and dressed in their finest, the students climbed aboard the bus that was to take them to their selected college. Excitement was high.

The Experience: Each College hosted their group in a different way but all provided a wonderful, never to be forgotten experience for these youngsters. Many had never been to a college. Most had no idea about the possibility of attending one. They all came back with an enthusiastic attitude about a future that included the possibility of attending a college. They were ready to save their money and study harder to improve their grades. Their teachers, some who were skeptical before the visit, were now in full support. They reported a positive change for learning for many of their students.

Post Visitation Sharing: Students couldn't wait to relate their experiences. Just looking at the sparkle in their eyes as they told their story was enough to make everyone realize how affective the visitation was. They all had an assignment to write a letter to their host at the college thanking them for the day. They did it with gusto.

The original GSA lobby was able to raise the standards and performance levels for many students and it still does.

"Early Birds", Heart Attack to Fitness:

On June 30, 1973, I suffered a heart attack that would change my life. Things like heart attacks tend to do that. Why now when things were going so well? I became obsessed with the "Why". I read articles and books about it. I listened to radio and television programs. Until the heart attack I had no idea how many of the people I knew had one or knew someone who did. They all had advice that they were anxious to share. I listened to all of them. I learned about diet, exercise and cholesterol both good and bad. I learned about stress factors and blood pressure. I took seriously the evils of smoking and quit immediately. Most of all, I learned about causes, early intervention and prevention.

Many of the articles I read and doctors I spoke to talked about early intervention. I should have begun to pay attention long before that fateful day when my body was getting ready to fail me. I ignored factors like family history, cholesterol, blood pressure, how cigarettes were damaging my arteries and the lack of physical conditioning. I thought I was too young to worry about those things! As it turned out, I should have worried about them even before I reached my teens.

How could I turn this knowledge into something positive? While recuperating in the hospital and at home, I had plenty of time to think about all the things flooding through my mind. I thought about my own children and how my experience could help them. Along with me, they learned about foods that increased both good and bad cholesterol. They learned that cigarettes were poison as my wife and I became intolerant of those who smoked. One of the first rules we instituted was No Smoking in the House!

Helen, my wife read cookbooks and labels on packages to find the best heart friendly recipes. We all changed the way we ate and lived.

But why stop with just my kids and my family? As an elementary school principal, I could pass this knowledge on to the kids who attended our school. That was how I could turn lemons into lemon aide. I had the knowledge, credibility and the opportunity to do some good for others.

Too many of our fifth grade students were well on their way toward becoming obese adults. I spoke to my two physical education teachers, Lilka Lichtneger and Rich Rowcroft about a conditioning program for fifth grade students who showed the symptoms we were looking for. They were obesity, lethargy and poor physical conditioning.

They were both interested in the project. Lilka, Rich and I discussed the, who, what, when and where of a program that could reach the fitness goals that we set. Our task was to find those children who were already at risk for a future heart attack and turn their lives around. After much discussion, we arrived at a plan.

We would identify a dozen or so ten year olds who were overweight and out of shape. The test was simply to find those fifth graders who could not run, jog, or walk a half-mile in eight minutes. They would be our target group. We talked to their teachers and watched their behaviors. Most of them exhibited a lack of self-confidence. Their weight problem was not just physical it was affecting their every-day lives. Some were the butt of hurtful comments or worse, just ignored by their peers.

We set up a program that would meet their needs while not embarrassing them. They would come to school an hour before the opening bell. The first half hour they would exercise and the second half hour they would eat a healthy breakfast. During their breakfast Lilka and Rich would talk to them about living healthy. Lilka and Rich loved the project. Every time we met to discuss new ideas, they came with more information and greater enthusiasm.

At one of these sessions, we came up with a name for the kids "The Early Birds". The PTA purchased bright yellow T-shirts for the kids with "JFK Early Birds" written in bold letters across their chest. This was going to work! All it needed was to get all the pieces to mesh. That was my job. John at the bus garage agreed that he could and would transport the kids to school an hour earlier than the rest of the students. The cooks who came in early to prepare lunch agreed to prepare an "Early Bird" breakfast. PTA agreed to purchase the breakfast ingredients.

When we had the plans and agreements all set we took it to our Central Administrators. They liked the idea and gave us the go ahead. That left the parents and last but most important of all, the kids to come on board.

I called each of the parents of the targeted kids and set up an individual appointment with them. At the meeting, I explained the reasons for and the benefits of the program. Their children would hear about blood pressure, exercise and weight factors. "Now was the time to prevent a heart attack" was my thrust. Ten of the twelve parents agreed to support the plan providing their child agreed.

Lilka, Rich and I met with the ten children and explained what The Early Birds would be doing. They would meet three mornings each week for the next twenty weeks to exercise, eat a healthy breakfast and learn about fitness. They all agreed!

We advised parents to consult with their child's doctor regarding the program. The doctors not only agreed with the benefits of the program they offered their support.

On the first day, each participant received a notebook that became their diary. They were shown how to record their at-rest pulse rate, blood pressure and weight. They wore their "Early Bird T" shirts with pride. They were filled with expectations and excitement.

For the first ten minutes, they shared their experiences related to fitness. For the next twenty minutes, the Early Birds were involved in a warm up exercise followed by an exercise that raised their pulse rate to their pre-established fitness level. They recorded the information in their diary.

After properly warming down it was time for breakfast. Low-fat milk, low sugared cereal and fruit made up much of the breakfasts. During breakfast the group's conversation focused on fitness and having them feel good about themselves.

Week after week, their marked improvement was noted in their diary. It was as if their body was just waiting for this new regiment and was happy to respond with better numbers for their pulse rate, blood pressure and weight. The marked improvement noted in their diaries encouraged them to work even harder.

Their entire demeanor changed. Lethargy was replaced with enthusiasm. They earned praises and felt proud of their achievements. Their schoolwork improved as noted by their teachers. Best of all, their classmates showed them respect. In fact, many were jealous of "The Early Birds". Can you imagine being jealous of waking up an hour earlier to come to school and exercise?

Word of the success of the program got around the community. People expressed many positive feelings about John F. Kennedy School's new program for kids who needed help

.

This was too good to keep to ourselves. I called Newsday, our local newspaper and told them what we were doing. They were interested and sent a reporter to cover the event. The article appeared on their obituary page and soon exploded all over the media. Radio stations around the country called for interviews. ABC came to school to photograph a session. The program was aired during prime time.

Coincidently, Time-Life Publication was doing an article that turned into a book about, The Healthy Heart. They sent photographers and a writer to get the story. The Early Birds, Rich, Lilka and I, were interviewed and photographed. The ten-page article filled with photographs and interviews appeared in their hard covered book entitled, The Healthy Heart. We all became celebrities!

There is hardly anything in life that can give you more pleasure than knowing that you have made a positive difference in someone's life. I think teachers and principals have the opportunity to experience those feelings more than in any other profession.

When opportunity strikes turn lemons into lemonade.

Chapter 11

Taking a Stand

What is a "Team Player"?

The Superintendent & the Smoking Room

Periodically the Superintendent met with the principals to discuss issues and ideas. I was a newly appointed Principal and very pleased to be part of these meetings. The principals would sit around a table. The Superintendent would tell us about an idea he had that he was planning to present to the Board. Then he would ask the principals for our opinion.

The issue for this day was to set aside a room in the high school for students who smoked. It seems kids were smoking all over the building and making a mess. The custodians came up with the idea to have one room set aside for those students who would use only that room in which to smoke.

As you have deduced, this was long before all smoking was banned in schools. This incident occurred shortly after the Surgeon General declared "smoking cigarettes to be harmful". The plan was to only allow those students who brought a permission note from their parents that indicated that they approved of the plan for their child.

I could just imagine how much pressure the parents would be under to sign that permission slip. In addition, wasn't this having the school give tacit agreement to having kids smoke? The curriculum included the requirement to teach a unit at each grade level starting in Kindergarten regarding the evils of smoking and now we are giving license to it?

The Superintendent, as was his custom, opened the discussion with why he liked the plan. Then he went around the table asking for each person's opinion. Principal after principal agreed with the Superintendent's plan. Then it was my turn. I expressed three things that bothered me about the plan.

First the pressure that would put on the parents who were trying to do the right thing. Second the Surgeon General's recent declaration explaining the health problems brought about by smoking cigarettes. Third, and most important, was the fact that we were teaching the evils of smoking but giving it tacit approval by designating a room specifically for smoking.

The Superintendent glared at me. That ended the asking for opinions for that issue. We went on to other topics. I felt uncomfortable. After the meeting, a fellow principal advised me to go along with the Superintendent when he proposed an idea. "Even if I differ?" "Especially!" said my mentor. "In order to be considered a team-player, go along to get along."

My mistake was to think that the Superintendent was asking for honest input. I made a promise to myself that whenever I asked for input I would not express my opinion first. I would honor any person whose opinion differed from mine. If I didn't want to hear an opinion that differed from mine, I would not ask for an opinion. To me a team player is one who says what he or she thinks and after the decision is made, goes along and supports it. It was a good lesson.

The June Fair

The elementary schools in this district had a tradition of conducting a very elaborate fair in June to mark the end of another school year. The newly erected John F. Kennedy School was certainly going to follow that tradition. Preparations were begun in early May to make this a gala event. Each class planned an event or a booth that would be showcased on that day.

The PTA supplied food, beverages and a multitude of prizes for the variety of games that would be played by children and adults. Parents joined the fun and added to the things to do. It was a very exciting time. The only thing we hoped for was good weather. But even if it rained and we could not have it outside we had plans to take the whole thing into the gym and cafeteria. Not as much fun but still a great day. We figured all contingencies were covered.

The fair was scheduled for Saturday, June 8, 1968. Those of you who know your history know that date. It was the day that Robert F. Kennedy Jr. the senator from New York, was to be buried. Senator Kennedy was assassinated three days earlier on June 5th and the nation went into shock. Another Kennedy was murdered. On Thursday, June 6th, the principals met with the assistant superintendent to discuss a variety of issues. Our main concern was how we should handle this with the students.

After the meeting, the assistant superintendent and I spoke about the June fair that was only 2 days away. I was shocked at her suggestion that we go ahead with the fair. She said the children and their parents would be very disappointed after all the planning that had taken place if it was cancelled.

I told her that I couldn't imagine how we could run a fair at the same moment the assassinated senator from New York was being buried. I will never forget her next words. They were, "Senator Kennedy loved children and he would have wanted the fair to go on." I always wondered how people could know what dead people would have said. She flat out told me to go on with the fair. I told her that I would bring the matter to the PTA and staff.

When I got home that evening I spoke with my wife who had a much more level head than me. We discussed the issues including the fact that I did not yet have tenure. If I refused to go on with the fair would that jeopardize my continuance as a principal. That was a possibility. I thought about it the rest of the night.

My persistent thought was that the brother of John F. Kennedy, for whom the school was named, was going to be buried on the day of our gala June fair. I decided that I could not be there!

On Friday, June 7th I met with the PTA and staff. There was overwhelming agreement to sadly cancel the fair. Plans that had been made now had to be reversed. All the work and the impending joy came to a crashing halt. Sadness and shock prevailed. I met with the staff to discuss how they would address this tragedy with their students. What answers could we give youngsters that could explain their "whys"?

I then called the assistant superintendent and told her that we decided to cancel the fair. To her credit, she did not argue with the decision and I don't think it caused me any future problem. In fact, it may have set the tone for how I would make difficult decisions that would affect the school.

From Marching Band to Superintendent

Who would believe that someone could go directly from being the High School Marching Bandleader to the Superintendent of Schools? I know it is hard to believe but that is exactly what happened.

The story began when the marching bandleader claimed he should receive the same stipend for leading the band as the head football coach got for coaching the football team. In negotiation, the Board decided that the marching bandleader was not entitled to the same stipend as the football coach. The bandleader decided to quit leading the band! This set off a great amount of dissension in the school and the community. Sides were chosen and angers flared.

One thing led to another and the Band Parents Association, who favored the bandleader decided they could run their own members for the Board of Education and if they won a majority of the seats, they could "call the shots". They did and they won!

Once in power, they pressured the current Superintendent into resigning. Then, claiming to be doing a worldwide search for a new Superintendent, which in fact gave the bandleader time to get his Superintendent's license, the new board elevated the bandleader to the Superintendent's position. He may have been good as a marching Band Leader but he was not as a Superintendent. At his first meeting with the principals, he told us to either follow him or "Get your resumes together." Not a good way to begin and this was just the beginning.

His lack of experience was having a detrimental affect on the district. He made many mistakes in trying to make changes in the way the schools were to be run. He made unilateral decisions to show that he was in charge. His decisions were often contrary to what the principals advised but he was not to be stopped.

As principals, we decided not stand by and let this happen. The district had too good a reputation to let it be destroyed by his lack of experience. We met privately after school and discussed what we were able to do to right the situation. We spoke to our SAANYS attorney who said we could do some things to help get a different Board elected that could then deal with him. The attorney said he would help us in this endeavor while keeping us within the law. This became the goal for the principals.

We used every legal means to influence the next Board election. We did whatever we could to aid those candidates who were opposed to the new Superintendent. The campaign was long and heated but the day of the election finally came.

I waited at home near the phone to hear the results. When the phone rang, I held my breath. The simple message was "We won!" The Board configuration changed from 5-4 for the new Superintendent to 5-4 against him. These were the most difficult times and the most exciting times I have ever experienced. We joined together to save a district and won.

Nothing remains static. Situations can change over night. Be prepared!

Chapter 12

The Best Laid Plans Can Go Wrong

The New Special Class

My good friend and Assistant Superintendent called me near the end of the school year to tell me that the E.D. class would be housed in my school the following year. E.D. stood for Emotionally Disturbed. To this day, I cannot believe that was the name chosen and accepted for the class. But I digress. I already had three E.M.R. classes in the school. E.M.R. stood for Educable Mentally Retarded. That name didn't do much for me either. They were taught by three of the best teachers I ever saw. I will write more about them in the chapter titled, "Teachers Who Have the Magic".

For a good portion of the summer, I thought about where to locate this class of six, seven and eight year old children who had been adjudicated as Emotionally Disturbed. I figured that the E.M.R. kids and the E.D. kids could not mix so I decided to place them as far apart from each other as I could. That placed the E.D. kids in the Kindergarten wing just down the hall from my office. That wound up to be one of my worst decisions.

The class was equipped with desks and chairs, a portable black board, books, art supplies and a carpenter's workbench filled with tools that they brought from their other school. I wondered about the workbench but figured that the teacher knew what she was doing.

The teacher, it turned out, was a very loving, warm person. She truly loved each of her charges and believed that hugs and letting kids "express themselves" was the best ways to deal with their behavior problems. She was very well trained and had many years of experience with this type of child behavior. Who was I to differ with her methods?

One of the first indications I had that the location was wrong took place on the second day of school. While standing in what was known as the Kindergarten Hall I heard some angry screaming that included curses I had not heard since I left the army. The shouts were loud and clear and coming from the E.D. class. I rushed in, closed the door behind me and looked at the teacher to see what I could do to help restore order.

She was watching two kids go at each other with this diatribe. The other kids were watching or disinterested. The two kids were in each other's face venting their anger. The teacher was standing by watching. When she looked up and noticed me in the room she looked a little puzzled. I must have looked a lot puzzled. She told the kids to stop and take their seats so that she could speak to the principal. They did!

She then took me aside to talk to me about "Conflict Resolution". Her aim was to keep them from punching each other and it apparently was working. She let them scream and curse at each other as long as they did not physically fight.

What could I say? I told her that there were Kindergarten classes right next door and I would prefer them not learning that vocabulary just yet. She told me she understood and would close the door when this type of activity was going on.

I left the room figuring what I was going to say to the Kindergarten parents that were sure to call about the language their 5 year-olds heard coming from that room. As it turned out, no one called. They either didn't believe what their child said or the kids didn't talk about it. Whatever! I waited for the shoe to drop but it never did.

Of course, this was by no means the last episode I was to have with my new class. Everyone understood that if ever that teacher needed help I would drop everything, no matter what and get to her room.

One afternoon my secretary rushed into my office and said, "She needs you." I was off down the short hall to the room. I opened the door and witnessed bedlam. All the kids were screaming and running around the room. There were only eight but it seemed and sounded like 50. This kid had a hatchet in his hand and was chasing something on the floor. It was the class hamster, which had somehow gotten out of its cage. The hamster was running for its life and the hatchet bearing kid was looking to end its life. The other kids were rooting for the hamster and were cheering for it. The teacher was trying to reason with the culprit who was paying her no mind.

I took a deep breath and bellowed, "Everyone Freeze!" Fortunately, I was gifted with a very powerful, deep and when it was needed, threatening voice. I am sure the E.M.R. classes at the other end of the building heard me.

Everyone froze. All terrified eyes were on me. I'm not sure who the kids were more frightened of, the hatchet kid or me. After a few seconds I glared at the hatchet bearing kid and said in the same menacing voice, "Lay – the – hatchet – on – the – floor – and – step – back." I had learned that phrase in the army while on guard duty. Much to my delight, he did. It is a good thing because I didn't have a plan B. I was far too angry to ask the teacher for an explanation and I never did. I simply removed every tool from the workbench and gave them to the custodian. She too never said a word to me about my method.

Another incident

On another occasion, the E.D. class teacher called to tell me she would be absent the next day. I cringed! Back then principals called substitutes. This was the most difficult substitute assignment to cover. I would call a substitute from the list and promise a reward of three easy assignments for any day they served in the E.D. class. After a while even that didn't work. I had to beg them to please help me for just this one time.

On this occasion, I had all but exhausted the list of my tried and experienced subs, and was left with someone I did not know. After she accepted the job I told her about the class and that I would always be available if she needed any assistance. When she arrived, I showed her to the class, told her there were only eight students and where the intercom phone was if she needed me.

The morning passed without a call and I figured I was home free. Just like what happens right after commenting on how well traffic is moving on the Expressway when all traffic comes to an immediate halt around the next curve. I was punished. One should never say how well things are going on in that class. The call came right after lunch. I rushed in to find the new sub cowering in the corner of the room still clutching the intercom phone. The class was in riot form. Even my bellowing voice didn't work. By now, I had a plan B and put it into effect. I went to the blackboard and scratched the board with my fingernails making a screeching sound that sent chills through everyone's ears. That brought the riot to a halt. I was then able to get the class back to their seats and return them to acceptable behavior.

Note: If you can stand scratching on the blackboard it is very effective. The sound has the ability to stop whatever is going on at that moment. I have not tried it but I'm sure it would stop a charging Bull. I myself have to grit my teeth while doing it. After a few scratching episodes all I had to do was approach the board with my finger nails showing to get order. You never know what can work.

I told the sub that I would take the class and that she could go to the teacher's room to settle down. About twenty minutes later, she returned looking much more composed. I really did not think she would return to the class but she did. She blamed herself for letting things get out of control. I was very impressed and told her so. She in turn apologized for loosing her cool. That started a friendly conversation at the end of the day that turned into an interview. I called her often to sub and she got the next permanent teaching job and became one of our excellent teachers.

I could fill a book with tales of the happenings with that class.

Kindergarten Thanksgiving Day Luncheon

One November day the three Kindergarten teachers came to my office with a plan. The Kindergartens were half-day at that time. They asked if they could put their AM and PM sessions together for the day and prepare a Thanksgiving Day luncheon. The children would help plan their special Thanksgiving Day meal, buy the food at the local supermarket and prepare their feast.

I wholeheartedly supported the idea. These were three professional teachers and I knew they could handle their 160 children. My job was to get the approval of the bus garage to pick up both the AM and PM session children in the morning and get them all home in the afternoon. John was in charge of the district's busses and he loved to play a part in special events. He said, "Yes!"

Our kitchen manager chimed in and gave the teachers permission to use her facility. Then I had to get to the supermarket manager to ask for his approval. The market was just down the street so I walked over to it and spoke to the manager. He was very supportive and in fact invited us to come to the store before it opened so that the children could see how they set up for the day. Great!

Our wonderful PTA held a fund-raiser to defray the cost of the luncheon. Parents were happy to volunteer their help. We were good to go!

The day came and all the plans that were so carefully made, began to take shape. The busses containing all the Kindergarten children arrived at school on time. Teachers and parents escorted the children to their classrooms and began putting on their costumes. Some were Pilgrims and others were Indians. Having twice the number of excited students in each class made it a little hectic but the teachers and parents were very able to maintain order.

I was given the honor of leading this group to the supermarket. I felt like the Pied Piper leading 160 costumed children down the street. People living on the street looked out their windows or stood by their doors to watch this passing parade.

Minutes later we arrived at our destination. The supermarket manager was waiting to greet us. I could see by the broad smile on his face that he was as happy to see us, as we were to be there. He outlined the itinerary that he had prepared for us. It included how the registers work, the reasons for where various items were placed and the behind the scenes areas. He then handed out gifts for everyone. It was getting better by the minute. We toured the store and stopped at the produce department where the fruit and vegetable person showed everyone how to choose melons. We went to the dairy department where the adults tasted some cheese. We did the whole works.

The last place on the agenda was the butcher's area. We squeezed into the preparation room that was not made to hold this many people. Being the first in I found myself plastered against the back wall. Large stainless steel knives and hatchet like implements hung from racks. There were thick tables with various cutting tools on them. I started to feel a little uncomfortable. Was it the heat or the room?

Waiting for us was the butcher dressed in his starched, white apron that had a bit of claret showing. You could see that he was looking forward to this moment and had prepared his talk and demonstration for us. It was likely his first teaching experience and he was going to make the most of it. He held up shrink-wrapped packages of steak, chicken and lamb chops. He showed us where to look for the price and weight on each package. Then he said, "See this package? It contains lamb chops that you may have for dinner tonight. But I am going to show you how it gets to be lamb chops."

With that, he opened the large refrigerator door and rolled out, on a trolley, the carcass of a whole lamb hanging from a hook. With a mighty effort, he hoisted the carcass off the hook and placed it on a table that contained a large band saw. As soon as I realized what he was about to do, I tried to stop him but by then he had turned on the switch and the screeching sound made by the saw obliterated my voice. The saw made hideous noises as it cut through flesh and bone. The noise was ear piercing! The butcher was cutting into that lamb carcass and was going to show these kids how lamb chop packages were made.

I watched the expression on the faces of the children. Some started to whimper others cried at the thought that Mary's Little Lamb was being made into chops. Everyone except the butcher was getting upset. Teachers and parents looked to me for direction. Being crammed against the wall, I was unable to get the butcher's attention. He continued to make his cuts. I waved my arms wildly and finally the butcher looked up. I could tell from the look on his face that he had no idea of the affect this carving up of the lamb was having on the kids and adults watching him. When he saw their expressions and my waving arms he shut the saw down. It took about a minute but it seemed like ten for the blade to stop moving and finally silence the screeching noise it had been making.

Parents and teachers were consoling the kids who looked the most horrified. When the butcher looked up and saw what was happening he realized what he had done. He tried to apologize but all everyone wanted was to get out of that butcher shop. I thanked him and assured him that everything was going to be all right once we got back to school.

The rest of the morning went without incident. The teachers purchased the food for the luncheon and prepared it for the Indians and Pilgrims.

Fortunately, he had not demonstrated with a turkey so the plans for the luncheon could continue. But the enthusiasm of the morning seemed to have been diminished. Many children claimed not to be hungry for lunch.

I wonder how many vegetarians were made that day?

Chapter13

Teaching is Harder Then You Think

The Psychologist & The First Grade Teacher

In the late 60s and early 70s, many psychologists and child development experts took the position that kids would behave properly if they felt loved and would misbehave if love was denied them. Often a teacher who sent a child to see the school psychologist was told that the most important thing is for the child to be feeling loved and being wanted. This brings me to the next story.

A brand new psychologist with no classroom experience was assigned to our school. He was certainly into the ideas of the day that said love was the answer for most children with discipline problems. The following incident occurred.

Helen Kroupa an outstanding first grade teacher with many successful years of experience was having a great deal of trouble with a particular boy in her class. He was disrupting lessons and continually creating a disturbance. She spoke to the boy and to his mother and they both tried different ways to get him to behave. Nothing worked! She came to me for advice. We decided that I should observe his behavior first hand.

The next day I sat in on her class. She used all kinds of ways to get him to pay attention but none lasted for more than a minute or two. Even with my presence, the boy acted out. After a short while I had seen enough. At our conference, Helen and I agreed to have the boy seen by the school psychologist. The parents were consulted and agreed to their child being tested by the psychologist. Helen wrote up a referral and gave it to the psychologist.

A few days later, the psychologist met with the boy. He talked to him, tested him and played games with him. When he spoke to me he reported that the boy was very bright and a pleasure to talk with. He found no attention problems and felt he just needed to feel wanted in the class. He intimated that the teacher was not handling the situation correctly. I explained that she was an excellent teacher and hardly had any discipline problems that she could not control in the past but the psychologist persisted. He showed Helen his findings and advised her of how love was the answer. She was not impressed!

It happened some weeks later that this same first grade teacher had an afternoon appointment and requested that I get her a substitute for the day. When we both determined that she did not have to leave until after lunchtime, I got an idea. How about asking the psychologist to take the class for the hour and a half that remained in the afternoon? He would get some classroom experience and we would not have to get a substitute. That sounded good to her and to me, so I put the idea to him. He was reluctant at first but agreed that it would be a new experience and could help him better understand the classroom setting.

He had a week to prepare his lesson. His wife, who was a first grade teacher in another district, could help him with his plan. The day before the lesson he came to show me his plan. He planned to play a piece of classical music and have the children draw how the music made them feel. I asked him if he thought the students could maintain interest in the one lesson for an hour and a half. He thought yes. I told him to go for it.

The day came and he was a little nervous but anxious to go. I walked him to the class and introduced him to the students telling them that he would be their teacher for the afternoon. With that, Helen and I walked back to my office.

It did not take fifteen minutes when the intercom buzzer rang. My secretary answered and said it was the psychologist. He was having trouble with a boy who was totally disrupting his lesson.

I told my secretary to have him fill out a referral and send it to the psychologist. I let him sweat for about five more minutes before I went to the room and restored order. He looked pale and shaken. He tried to explain that the boy who was the problem for the teacher could not differentiate between their one-on-one sessions together and his role as the classroom teacher. I finished the day.

Weeks later he came to me and said that the more he thought about the experience the more he realized that it was a valuable lesson for him. We joked about it for years. As a result, he became a better School Psychologist and helper for teachers.

Basic Training vs. a Fourth Grade Class:

I graduated from college during the Korean Conflict. I fully expected to be called to service shortly after graduation. For some reason that I did not question, the call did not come. Instead, I took a teaching job and waited for the draft to catch up with me. Or not!

My assignment was with 36 fourth graders. The students were bright and eager to learn and I was eager to teach them. I enjoyed the fourth grade curriculum because, among other things, it called for a lot of writing. I had the kids start a journal, which meant that I had a lot of writing to read and correct.

After teaching from nine to three and spending an additional 3 hours correcting and making suggestions for their compositions I had just enough energy to read the newspaper, eat dinner and get to sleep. Friends would ask me to meet them after work but I was too tired. For a while I thought there was something wrong with me. I was very active in sports while at college and did not feel half as tired at the end of the day as I was feeling after a day's teaching.

I finished my first year and started my second when the draft caught up with me. A notice came for me to report to Fort Dix in December of my second year. I gave notice to the Superintendent, said goodbye to the kids, put my affairs in order and reported for duty.

The first eight weeks in the army were dedicated to basic training. That entailed getting up at 5 AM for some brisk physical training, eating breakfast with 500 guys in a battalion mess hall, making up my bunk and then falling out to start the day's activities.

That consisted of long marches, firing weapons, digging holes, cleaning my rifle and getting ready for dinner. If I had no additional duty after dinner, the guys and I would leave the barracks and go out. As tired as I was physically, I was not as tired as I was at the end of a school teaching day. How could that be? Very simple! Teaching is very hard! Keeping a class of students busy and interested takes a great deal of planning and hard work. If I had not experienced it I would never have believed it.

After serving for two years I was discharged and resumed my teaching career. Once again I experienced the tiredness at the end of a day's teaching. I realized that I could use some help and received it whenever I could get it. The best example of this follows:

I was dating a teacher named Helen Klinger at the time. On one particular date, I brought some compositions my students had written so that she could help me with grading them. Not very romantic I admit but very different and helpful. In any case, it worked for both of us. Shortly afterwards she agreed to marry me. Be aware that I am not suggesting this is a way to a woman's heart. Throughout my career as a teacher and administrator, my lovely wife has continued to be my most valuable asset.

Covering A Special Education Kindergarten:

The art teacher came to my office one day to tell me that she would be absent for the next few Thursdays. She explained that a student in the self contained Kindergarten Special Education class had Fifths Disease which was very detrimental to her pregnancy and she would have to stay home on the days she had that class.

I realized that she would need to take off many days before and after giving birth thereby losing the sick days she had accumulated through the years. It seemed like a waste to lose a whole day for just one class period. I volunteered to take that class if she would give me a lesson plan to follow. She was very appreciative and I could tell that she had told other members of the staff what a nice guy I was. I was very pleased with myself.

The day came and I walked into the classroom armed with the lesson plan. The kids were very happy to see me. There was no concern on their face or their behavior that showed they were impressed that the Principal was going to be their teacher for this lesson. The classroom teacher introduced me to the class and told them to "listen and behave". Little did I know how important those words would be.

The lesson involved small motor control using a pair of scissors to cut out shapes that were to be pasted onto some construction paper. I handed out some colored paper and a pair of safety scissors to each of the 11 students and began to explain what they were to do. I wasn't 10 seconds into explaining the lesson when one student began cutting the paper.

Mistake # 1! I should have explained before handing out the material! I walked over to the student and told him to put the scissors down until I had finished the instructions.

Mistake #2! By the time I got compliance from that child three others had started cutting. Realizing that it was no use, I continued the explanation for those who were still paying attention and told them to get started. Now remember this was a class of 5 year olds with learning problems. Off they went, cutting, tearing, crumpling and throwing. This one asked for my help, then that one, then another before I had even reached the first questioner.

I began to perspire. I looked at my watch and realized that only 7 minutes had elapsed. There were 28 minutes to go before I could be rescued by the classroom-teacher. I thought to myself that if she was even one minute late I would be very upset. That's how nuts I was. At one point, I looked around for a camera that must have been placed in the room recording my every move. I thought Allen Funt was about to enter and say, "Smile, you're on candid camera." I ran around like the proverbial chicken looking at my watch as the minute hand hardly moved.

At minute 25, I realized that all the effort I was making to gain control of the situation was futile and the best I could do was to sit back and let the kids do what they would. The kids were having a grand old time so as long as no one was injured I would let the good times roll.

The classroom teacher returned on time and saw how flushed I was. She asked if I was okay. "Fine" I said as I said "Goodbye" to the kids and rushed out the door. Arriving at my office, I closed the door, sat at my desk and thought about what went wrong.

Mistake #3! I was not and never have been an art teacher or a Kindergarten teacher. A good thing that came out of the experience was that the staff knew about it and appreciated my valiant effort. So maybe it was worth the disaster.

The lesson that came out of the experience was that you should stick to what you know.

Try Kindergarten For A Morning

One morning one of my best Kindergarten teachers came to my office. She closed the door as she entered and immediately began to cry. This was not going to be a usual problem. I handed her some tissues, gave her a glass of water and waited for her to compose herself. When she did, she began to tell me about her problem. It had to do with her marriage. She was married about 5 years and had given birth to three children one after the other. They obviously needed a great deal of attention. The added expenses of having three children required that she continue to earn a salary but she was having trouble doing both jobs well.

It seems that her husband who had a labor intensive job that called for long hours expected his three children to be fed, bathed and ready for bed by the time he came home late in the evening. In addition, he expected dinner to be ready for him after he got home and washed away the grime and sweat that his work produced. She told me through tears and exasperation that her husband said, "Your job can't compare to mine. You work six hours a day, five days a week from nine to three with an hour for lunch and a break every day. I work 10 hours a day, six days a week lifting and carrying."

Those of us who have taught have heard these words for as long as we have been in the profession from those who are not in the profession. "Summers off, numerous holidays, short hours…"

It so happens that I knew her husband. He played shortstop for the same team as my son and I attended many of their baseball games. I often spoke with him and we had a good relationship. I considered him to be a nice young man.

A strange idea popped into my head. It was unorthodox to be sure but fitting for the problem. I suggested to the teacher that her husband come to school on his day off and teach her Kindergarten class for part of the morning. She thought about that for a moment and said, "He will never go for that." I told her to bring him to the next PTA meeting and I would have a go at it. Sure enough, he came to the next PTA meeting and I was able, after chiding him mercilessly, to arrange for him to come to the school during his day off.

The day came and there he was ready to prove that he could handle this new assignment. I almost could not contain myself imagining how the kids in the Special Education Kindergarten class would react to this new man who was going to be their teacher for a while. I walked him to the classroom and introduced him to the class. The kids were very pleased. I told him that it was required that I be right outside the door if he needed any help. He assured me that this would be "A piece of cake".

You know what happened next. The kids loved him and were all over him as he tried to read them the story he had prepared. He tried to peal them off and get some order to no avail. In his frustration, he yelled for them to take their seats. Some did not pay any attention. Some went to their seats and some started to cry. That did it! He came to the door and begged me to bring his wife back to the classroom.

When she returned I walked her husband back to my office. He was shaken and I told him not to feel too badly. I told him that teaching was a lot harder than it seems to people who have not experienced it. I told him how I found my experience during Basic Training to be in many ways easier than teaching. I do not know if I convinced him but it surely made a dent in his thinking.

On Becoming "A Principal"

Helen's Grandmother said up front what most people thought at the time.

The first time she met me after Helen and I became engaged, Grandma asked, "What does he do for a living?"

Helen, "He's a school teacher."

Grandma, "A school teacher? For a smart girl I thought you would do better!"

That was welcome to the family from Grandma.

In our society, be it then or now, money trumps most everything else! Teachers were certainly not going to become affluent as I started my career. My starting salary in 1952 was $3,000 for the 10 months that made up the school year. That was 7% more than most surrounding districts paid but, it was not enough for me to live on for the 12 months that make up a year. The summer months that non-teachers point to as a benefit that teachers have were spent on finding a summer job that would tide me over until the check that I would receive at the end of September could be used to pay off debts incurred during those lean summer months.

One of the things that money determines is esteem. My meager teacher's salary seemed to determine what people thought of me. What's more, the elementary grade level I taught didn't do much for their view of my esteem. Men who teach at the elementary level are considered by many to be among the least important. College professors are pretty high when it comes to esteem. It's not the money as much as the thought that they must be super smart. Coming down the ladder of esteem is the high school teacher. They teach young, soon to be adults a subject for which they must be experts. As an added attraction, there is more opportunity for them to become the head of a department, a coach or even an administrator.

I taught fifth grade for thirteen years and loved it. I thought what I did was important even if others did not. They all told me how important my job was but I didn't get the impression they thought much of my opinions.

One day everything changed! I was selected to be the Principal of an elementary school. I told the good news to my family and friends. I was no longer considered to be a teacher. I was now a Principal! The very next day, family and friends who knew me for years looked at me differently. Now my opinions were sought after. And not just with questions referring to education but the economy, health, restaurants you name it. Wasn't I the same person as I was the day before? Sure! But the day before I was a lowly teacher. Let me tell you a secret. Teaching, most of the time is far more difficult than being a Principal. It is the teacher as I have said many times that "delivers the service". They do this day in and day out.

As a Principal, I had other responsibilities. I set the tone for the building. I worked with teachers, parents and sometimes kids but I was not locked in a room with students who needed me for the entire time they were in class. If I felt like it, I could walk around and stop into any place in the building. I could close my door and read notices or make a phone call or just relax for a few minutes. Yes, there were times when things got crazy and for those times I earned my pay, but those times were few and far between. More importantly, I was there to help teachers deliver the service.

It is not as easy as it may seem! Try it before you get in over your head.

Chapter 14

The Perception Of A 5-Year-Old

My daughter, Susan, was a very happy Kindergarten student who could not wait to go to school in the morning. On that first day in September, my wife and I watched her get on the bus to begin her educational career. We then raced to the school to see her get off the bus. We were all very emotional about the experience. Each of our lives was about to change. We could not wait to hear about her day. Our son, David was also happy. He would be home for a few hours without having to share his mother's time with his sister. This was a happy time for everyone.

At the same time I was appointed Principal of an elementary school in another part of the district. The new job was to begin at the start of the second semester in January. Susan would be settled into her Kindergarten class when I would start my new assignment. Everything was working out well for our family. I couldn't wait to begin. That December we celebrated Susan's sixth birthday. One month later, I began my new job.

We always ate dinner together as a family. Each of us would have the opportunity to talk about our day. Quite suddenly, Susan's mood began to change. Strangely, Susan, who had loved Kindergarten for the first half of the year, began acting differently. From a happy, outgoing child she became sad and pensive. Both my wife and I recognized this change and probed Susan for answers. None were forthcoming. This went on for weeks to the point where my wife and I became quite concerned.

Then in February, she was back to her old, happy self again. Maybe now she could tell us what caused the changes in her behavior. We questioned her and found out the reason.

She told us that every day she went to school the principal would be standing out front to welcome all the children as they entered the building. Conversely, the principal would stand outside the building as the children got on their buses to go home. Then he would go back into the building. In Susan's six year-old mind that meant that when you were the principal you had to remain in school and never come home. She thought she would no longer see her Daddy. Her sadness came from this misconception! She was finally convinced when she saw me come home every day after school and she realized she still had her Daddy.

The lesson I learned was that Kindergarten children have many misconceptions about school. They are not little adults with the experience of adults. As children their world is filled with events that they interpret with the scant knowledge they possess, some correct, some way off. As a result, they make up some wonderful stories that come directly from their imagination. I loved it when Kindergarten teachers shared them with me.

I told the same story to the Kindergarten parents every year at the first PTA meeting. It goes like this. "If you promise not to believe everything your child says about us, we promise not to believe everything they say about you. When in doubt, check it out." This gets a laugh but also says "question before you draw conclusions".

I often wondered how many children come to Kindergarten that first day with fears and misconceptions that they are unable to explain. I think the answer is most. I remember that I never could sleep the night before the first school day. My mind would be racing with things that I had done to prepare for that next day. Did I forget something? Could I be better prepared? How would it go? That started at Kindergarten and continued until I was retired. I told this to parents, teachers and best of all, to kids. They looked at me and most often confessed that they too could not sleep the night before school began.

That first school day is one of the most important days of a student's school year! Treat it kindly!

Chapter 15

Testing vs. Assessment

This I believe:

Through the years, I have watched Standardized Tests retard learning. Well meaning people think that by giving a "fill in the bubbles" test at the end of a school year that would result in teaching and learning improvement. In spite of the fact that test scores have not improved through the years, Standardized Testing continues and proliferates. Do not misunderstand! Assessment is a valuable and important tool for learning but assessment and standardized tests bear little relationship to each other. What is the difference?

To begin with, Standardized Tests are given at the end of the school year. Assessment starts at the beginning of the year and is ongoing. That gives the teacher and the students the opportunity to look at what is known and what is unknown and correct misunderstandings.

What is the point of testing at the end of the year with a Standardized Test? It is too late to correct a student's mistakes. The test is over! Chances are the student doesn't even know which questions were correctly answered and which were incorrect. But who cares? The test is over! The only thing that counts are the final grades for the school.

The State Education Department (SED) created four levels for indicating proficiency. Students who score at level 1 are failing and must improve to at least the second level. Students at level 2 are below average and must strive to be gotten to level 3. The test given at the end of the school year determines the number of students in each category and what gets reported to the SED and to the media.

That's how the school, the principal and the teachers are evaluated. So… is that what this is all about? Is it the teachers, principals and the schools that are being evaluated? Then why the surprise when you hear that teachers are spending an inordinate amount of time teaching the test and principals are encouraging it?

If I know that my 180 days of teaching will be evaluated on the results of a single half-day's test you can bet that I will teach to that test!

Testing then determines the curriculum and **what** is taught! The type of test that is used as a measure determines **how** it is taught.

Therefore, a test that requires a short answer response of memorized facts will force the teacher to formulate lessons that seem best suited for passing that type of test.

The people who make up Standardized Tests must make them: Easy to administer; Easy to score; Easy to quantify (translate into percentages); Easy to disaggregate; and Easily disseminated.

The more emphasis placed on the scores of these tests the more teachers will concentrate their teaching time on them. As the pressure increases, we see improper methods used to get those ones and twos up to threes. By the way, spending time to get those threes to improve to fours often does not even count in the reporting. What does that tell you?

This leaves little room for things like field trips, putting on plays, doing projects that use the Internet and library resources just to name a few.

The best learning takes place when there is **a need to know** something. There are, "teachable moments" that come along from time to time. It borders on criminal to waste them. Thematic units that integrate the subject areas into a whole picture, produces an understanding for what is presented. The learning remains with the learner long after the lessons are over and the methods used for learning can be used for other learning. Students will have learned **how to learn!** Memorizing facts, in order to pass the "test" produces short-term learning that is very quickly forgotten just a few days afterwards. Is that learning?

Education and educators must change their paradigm. More of the same for students who are failing to begin with has only produced more failure. It also produces a sense of failure in the student's mind that reinforces failure.

Westward Expansion

My wife and I attended an open house at our daughter's junior high school. It was early in the school year as they usually are. We went from class to class following her schedule. Each teacher had 15 minutes to tell the parents what the year's curriculum would be. At one point we arrived at the Social Studies class. The teacher began speaking about her curriculum for the year. Coincidently the Cold War was in full force. To make matters more perilous, Arab countries and Israel were in the midst of what became known as the "Six Day War". World War 3 was a real possibility.

I raised my hand and in spite of an elbow in my ribs from my wife, asked if the current events would be discussed? The teacher's response has remained with me to this day. "I would love to take the time to discuss this but it will not be on the test and the Westward Expansion test is only 4 days away. The current topic is Westward Expansion." She was unfortunately correct and that was long before teachers and schools were held as responsible for test failures. Today poor test results could determine salaries or even school closures. Can you imagine what is to be stressed now?

I said nothing but it spoke loud and clear to me. How many "teachable moments", that time when interest is high, are lost in order to stay with teaching that which is determined by what will be on the test?

Biology Test Forgotten

I was scheduled to take a Biology test in college. It was about the Phyla of the plant kingdom. There were scores of terms and sequences that had to be memorized. I spent hours just before the test cramming these unfamiliar terms into my memory bank. When the time came to take the test, I walked into the room and did not speak a single word to anyone. I was actually afraid that if I opened my mouth all that I had memorized would fall out. I took the test and passed it but I am positive that if that same test were sprung on me a week later I would have failed it. Have you ever felt that way?

So what did I learn? I tested my short-term memory. A friend of mine who had a photographic memory could close his eyes and see the entire page of a book he had read. He got 100% on every test we took that required memory retrieval. For him it was like an open book test. For me the book was closed. Short-term memory is not learning but that is what short answer tests, test! Why memorize facts that can easily be looked up when needed? Google makes fact memorization obsolete. If its purpose is to improve memory, memorize a poem!

The M1 Pencil

The army has some interesting ways of solving problems. One of them is called, "the M1 Pencil". I was taking Basic Training at Fort Dix, New Jersey in December of 1953. The army rule stated that a trainee had to pass the proficiency test with the M1 rifle before he could be placed on guard duty. The sergeant made it clear that everyone had to pass the test and as an added incentive, anyone scoring expert would get a weekend pass.

On the given day, we marched out to the rifle range. Half the company was in the pits with the targets and the rest of us got ready to fire at the targets. We got to the range early in the morning. So early that the ground fog surrounded us and obscured the targets. We waited as long as we could because another company was scheduled to follow us. When it became obvious that the fog would not lift in time, the sergeant gave the order to "commence firing". But at what? We could not see the targets! "Point down range and start firing" was the order. So... we all fired off the clip of bullets we had been issued.

When we were all finished, we marched to the pits to change places with the other half who would be firing their M1 rifles at the invisible targets. I took my place where my target was located and to my surprise found that many of my bullets apparently hit the bull's-eye. I got a very high score! But how could that be? Well it turned out that the guys in the pits were instructed to punch holes in the target with a pencil and the guy who punched my holes was very generous.

When we returned to the barracks we were given our scores. Seeing that I had made "expert" I asked the sergeant for my weekend pass. He just glared at me! Obviously, the test was not valid but who cared? It was the results that counted. We had to pass so that we could be put on guard duty. Sound familiar? How many M1 pencils are used today?

Memorizing 25 spelling Words

As a fifth grade teacher, I was responsible to teach spelling. The spelling book contained 25 words for each weekly assignment. On Friday I recited the 25 words and the students were tested. 90% was the passing grade and most students passed. I came to find out however that the words that were spelled correctly on the Friday test were often misspelled only weeks later when they were used in a composition. What had the students really learned in the time spent to pass that Friday test? Was the time we spent on it worthwhile? I decided to find out.

On Monday, I tested the class on the 25 words for that week with no preparation. Call it a pre-test. There were many scores that fell below the 90% passing level. I followed the directions in the book for the next three days that would help students memorize the words for that week. I tested them again on Friday. Friday's test results were much better.

I recorded both scores and placed them in my desk drawer. One month later, I pre-tested the class again with no warning using the same 25 words. The scores were not much different than they were on that first Monday before any of the week's lessons. They were by no means as good as the Friday test results. How come?

I decided to try another way. On Thursday of a given week, I told the class to incorporate as many of that week's spelling words into a composition. Needless to say they were not permitted to look at their spelling books. The results for the spelling words for that week were not even as good as the test I sprung on them. Spelling seemed to have little relationship to writing. The cramming they did Thursday night seemed to be the main determiner for the grade they received on Friday's test. The good spellers did well and the poorer spellers who had passed the Friday tests did as poorly as ever.

I did this a few more times to be sure and the results remained constant. So... I asked myself, was the one hundred minutes per week spent on spelling worthwhile?

That was the case long before spell-check came onto the scene making the one hundred minutes spent teaching spelling even less important today. But, you know what? My first and third grade grandchildren are still spending twenty minutes a day on the subject and their mother drills them every Thursday night for that dreaded Friday test.

Take the Test Anyway

It was near the end of the school year. I was a fifth grade teacher getting ready to administer the California Test of Basic Skills (CTBS) to my students. Dr. Tom Feniger, my good friend and the school psychologist, came to my classroom with a young boy who had just moved into the district. We settled the new boy into a seat and then my friend asked me to come outside into the hall. There he told me that this boy could not read. He came from the city where he had a terrible time and was very worried about coming to a new school. He asked me to just let him finish the year in a friendly atmosphere and they would deal with his learning problems for next year. Fine!

Two weeks later I handed out the booklets and scoring sheets for the CTBS exam. Knowing the new boy could not read but not wanting him to stand out among his classmates, I gave him an answer sheet and booklet and told him to just fill in one circle for each question. I noticed that he did not even open the booklet to the correct page but that was just as well.

Then it came time to score the tests. I placed the scoring sheet over each student's answer sheet and counted the number of correct answers that showed through the openings. I came across the new boy's answer sheet and just for fun placed the scoring sheet over his answers. Low and behold, he had some correct answers. Sure, there were four possible answers for each question so he had a 1 in 4 chance of getting any question correct. So... where there were 24 questions he had a good chance of getting 6 correct by simply filling in all the bubbles. There was no penalty for an incorrect answer but there was for leaving an answer blank. That gave you no chance. Six correct answers scored him 2 years below grade level. On some of the sections he got lucky and did better than the odds and even scored only a half -year below grade level.

I showed the results to my Principal who was duly impressed with what I had accomplished in just 2 weeks. I then said, "Can you imagine what he would have scored if he was on the right page for the test?" I explained what I had done.

What a lesson I learned about taking and scoring a "Standardized Test"!

Chapter 16

A Bully Is A Bully Is A Bully

Three stories that shaped my behavior

Mateo

I was a teenager living in a tough neighborhood in Brooklyn, NY. Five of my best friends, who were Jewish, lived in the same four-floored apartment as me. There was a gang that lived down the street who preyed on any of us whenever they found one of us alone simply because we were Jewish.

I would look around carefully before reaching my apartment building to be sure they were not waiting for me as I came home from school. If I saw them, I would wait far enough away so that I could outrun them back to the safety of the high school. From time to time, I would not see them in time and then I would have to take their bullying that included taunts and beatings. Aside from hurting from the beating, I felt so ashamed of myself for being so helpless.

One day I was trapped by six of them at the entrance to my apartment building. I was terrified! Once again, I tried to use reason that sounded more like begging, to talk them out of beating me up. They started by taunting and were about to start taking turns hitting me when Mateo turned the corner and saw what was happening. Mateo was a few years older than me and serving in the Navy. We knew each other because when the "Big Guys" needed another person for stickball they would let me play.

Mateo told them to get lost and to leave me alone. The leader of the gang told Mateo to mind his own business. In one quick move,

Mateo reached into a nearby garbage can, pulled out a bottle, broke it on the rim of the can and put it up next to the leader's face. He said in an angry voice, "If you don't get lost even your mother won't recognize you." That was the end of the confrontation. The six backed away and the look of fright that was on my face disappeared and was relocated onto their faces. That was it! This group of bullies was afraid of this one ferocious looking guy who did not back down.

After thanking Mateo he told me that, "Bullies like to see fear on the people they intimidate. Just show them that you are not afraid and tougher than they are and they will look for someone else to bully". That was it! Bullies do not need to tangle with someone who will fight back. There are always others they can strike fear into and intimidate.

If one incident can change a life, this one did mine. I learned to change fear into anger. I practiced by looking in a mirror and looking tough! Whether a street gang or any other situation where I was up-against a bully I refused to be cowered. I let the bully know that he would pay a price for starting with the wrong guy. I'm not going to say that it never ended in a fight but the bully knew he was not going to walk away unscathed. I think of Mateo every time and silently thank him for the lesson he taught me that day. I in turn have taught that lesson to many others.

David

I came home from work one day to find my wife very upset and my son in tears. "What's happening?" My wife told me there was a big kid in school who bullied other kids and had threatened to beat up my son David the next day. I thought by moving to the suburbs my kids would not experience bullying. Of course, I was wrong! Having been a teacher and Principal for many years I had dealt with many of these bullies. But here was my kid who his mother taught not to fight, being bullied and afraid of going to school. My wife gave the problem to me to solve.

David and I went to his room where I related the story of how a guy named Mateo taught me how to deal with bullies. I said, "First, don't try to talk your way out of it. A bully sees that as fear and that makes him feel even tougher. If he is out to beat you up he will do it anyway. Learn to turn your fear into anger! Who does this bully think he is? He is tangling with the wrong guy! The bully has to know this by what he sees in your facial expression and what you do. Practice by looking in a mirror at a menacing expression you put on your face. If it scares you, it is right. Go straight up to him first thing tomorrow morning, point your finger at his face and with that look on your face tell him his mother won't recognize him when he gets home after your fight." My son was shocked but he listened.

This will work in most cases but sometimes the bully needs to be shown. When you know you will be in a fight, get the first punch in and keep swinging. Someone will break up the fight and you will not get hurt any more than if you had let him hit you without hitting back.

I left David practicing to toughen himself up and went down to the kitchen. My wife asked me what I told David. When I told her she was appalled. "How could you?" You can imagine the rest of the argument. But the deed was done!

I couldn't wait to get home the next day to hear how my advice had gone. There was my smiling wife, my happy son and a boy who turned out to be the bully. It seems that after David put on that menacing face and threatened to beat him up, the bully said it was just a misunderstanding and chose to withdraw his threat. They shook hands and became friends.

Danny

Bullies often make their way to the principal's office. It is usually after all efforts to stop their misbehaviors have failed. Too often, having the principal reprimand the bully gives him bragging rights among his gang of friends.

Danny was a good-sized fifth grader who was what his teachers considered to be, "a good kid". He did his work and never bothered anyone. A Bully in his class decided that he could intimidate Danny and that he was the kind that would not fight back. The Bully began taunting Danny and when he saw he could get away with that he began pushing him around.

I met both of them one day when they were both sent to my office for fighting on the playground during recess. I gave time to both of them to tell their story. The Bully was brazenly telling a story of how "Danny started it." How many times had I heard that? Danny was fighting back tears as he told his side of the story. He too claimed that he did nothing to start the fight. I told both of them that I would look further into the matter and let them know my decision.

That day I spoke with their teachers. All of them told me that the Bully was always bullying others and that lately he was picking on Danny. I had both boys returned to my office and spoke to them one at a time. I told both of them what their teachers said about them. I told Danny I was sorry for what he was going through with this Bully. I told him that I had suffered a similar situation when I was his age and that I would let the Bully know that he would be punished if his misbehavior continued.

I then brought the Bully into my office and told him the negative things his teachers said about him. We talked about his reputation and how when a boy gets a bad one he often will be blamed for any fight even if it was not his fault. "Once you get a bad reputation, it is very difficult to get rid of so you would be wise to start changing it now". I got the feeling that my words were falling on deaf ears. Talking to a Bully has little chance of changing his behavior. But I gave it a try and for the moment that was all I could do.

One day Danny's grandmother came to my office. She told me that Danny was afraid to go to school because of a Bully who was intimidating him. We spoke about what I could do but that my punishing the Bully might not resolve the problem. She asked what she could do? I told her there was one sure way to stop a Bully and that was to stand up to him. I told her a little of my story and how I had advised my son to deal with his Bully. She was a little taken back when she realized that my advice was for Danny to punch the Bully as hard as he could the next time he was being bullied.

One day, a few months later both boys were sent to my office for fighting. This time the Bully was in tears and Danny was standing tall. It turns out that after our conversation Danny's grandmother registered him in a boxing class at the "Y". This time when the Bully started taunting Danny he got his nose bloodied. I spoke to each boy individually. To the Bully I said, "I guess Danny started fighting back." The Bully acknowledged that it was not a good idea to fight with Danny.

Next, I brought Danny into my office. He told me what his grandmother said after our meeting and that he was taking boxing lessons that taught him how to defend himself. With the door closed, I told him, with a wink, that I would have to reprimand him for fighting on the playground but that he would not be punished. However, it would be best if he left my office looking like he had been punished.

From time to time, I would ask their teachers how things were going? They all said Danny was still a good boy but had changed for the better. As for the Bully, he stopped picking on Danny but found others to intimidate. He was sent to my office on many occasions. I spoke with his parents who claimed that their son told a different story and that he was the one picked on. I could not convince them otherwise. The best I could do was to keep him off the playground for a few days as punishment when he was in a fight.

Not all Bullies are kids. Some grow up to be bullies at home, in the workplace and whenever they can intimidate others. The same principles apply to those who like to see fear in others.

The best way I know of to deal with Bullies is to make them realize that they chose the wrong person to try to intimidate.

Chapter 17

A Promise Is A Promise

The Nicks & The Celtics

Those who remember the year 1969 would agree that it was the greatest year for New York sports fans. It was also the year that my son turned eight and became an avid sports fan. To make matters more interesting it was the first year he had a male teacher. Mr. Carbrave and my son David were both Knick fans and talked about the games throughout the season. David could not wait to get to school to talk to Mr. Carbrave about the Mets, Jets and Knicks. They really bonded and I am sure that David's interest in basketball was enhanced by their mutual enjoyment for this very successful season.

As the season progressed it became evident that the Knicks with Frazier, Reed, DeBusschere, Bradley and Barnett were going to make it to the finals. Sure enough, they won the series that made them the Eastern Division Champs. At the same time, the Los Angeles Lakers with Jerry West and Wilt Chamberlain were winning the Western Division. The two teams, one from the West Coast and the other from the East Coast were going to battle it out for all the marbles. How exciting!

The teams split the first two games that were both played in New York. We could not watch them because home games were not televised locally at that time. The only games that were going to be televised back to New York were those that were played in Los Angeles where they began at 7:00 PM. 7:00 PM in Los Angeles is 10:00 PM in New York! Surely, that was too late for an eight year old to stay up to watch and then go to school the next day.

Game three was played in Los Angeles. David had no idea about the time difference. He only knew that he wanted to see the game. He begged me to let him watch the game. How could I refuse him? He had become such an ardent fan. He knew all the players and their numbers. He knew statistics for each player that really impressed me. On the other hand, how could I let him stay awake this late on a school night? I could be arrested!

I came up with what I thought was a good plan. I promised to let him watch the game if when he came home from school on the night of the game he would take a long nap. I mean really sleep for three hours. If he did that, I promised I would let him watch the game. I felt pretty good about my plan because I figured there was no way he would take that nap so I would have a good reason to get out of my promise.

The day came. David came home from school and went directly to his room. I waited for about half an hour and went to his room to check to see if he was sleeping. Sure enough he was. He slept for 3 hours! I woke him at six for dinner. He ate and did his homework. By Ten O'clock, he and I were ready to watch the game together as promised. My wife was incredulous! "Do you know he has to go to school tomorrow?" "I know, I know but I made him a promise." The look she gave me said it all but I was stuck.

The game was exciting from the opening tip off. The teams were evenly matched and the lead changed hands many times. Finally half time came. It was very late and I was very tired. Remember he took a nap, I hadn't. I looked at David and suggested that we both should go to sleep. "But Dad you promised" said David with pleading eyes. How could I do anything but agree and we settled in to watch the second half together.

Now picture this. It was well after midnight. Dave DeBusschere hit a jump shot with 3 seconds left on the clock that put the Knicks ahead by two points. The Lakers had used up all their times out and had to take the ball out in their end of the court. Just 3 more seconds and the game would be over. We would have won and we could both go to sleep.

Wilt Chamberlain in-bounded the ball to Jerry West, one second gone! West dribbled past Walt Frazier, two seconds gone! Then, from 60 feet out, West let fly a desperation shot. The buzzer rang as the ball made its way toward the rim. Can it be? Yes, the ball found its way through the rim! The two points (before the three point rule) tied the game and it would have to go into a fifteen minute overtime period. It was already the next day. I will spare you the details of the overtime period. The Knicks won! David and I could at last get to bed but who could sleep?

Somehow, I got through the next day and could not wait to get home and catch up on the sleep I had missed the night before. At about Four O'clock, the phone rang. It was David's teacher Mr. Carbrave. He got right to the point. He was calling to confirm what David could not wait to tell him about his watching the game the night before. He laughed and just wanted to hear it from me that David had made up the story about watching the entire game. After all, even Mr. Carbrave had not watched the entire game.

I sheepishly confirmed that in fact David and I had watched the entire game together. Needless to say, David never told Mr. Carbrave he had taken a three-hour nap before the game. I thought about telling him about the nap but decided it would sound like a lame excuse. I simply said that I had made a promise and…

A promise is a promise!

Chapter 18

Breaking Down Barriers

The First Check

This story may easily be misconstrued. It is important to know that it took place in the '60s and '70s when principals were feared. I am not sure it would play out the same today. But here goes.

In my district, new teachers were all interviewed and hired by the Superintendent. I usually met them just a few days before the start of the term. I was introduced to them for the first time as their Principal. I could see by the expression on their face and the way they spoke, that they were nervous in my presence. That was not the kind of relationship I wanted to have with them. I made an effort to get them to relax even though I knew that they were still very nervous talking with the "Boss".

They started work and after two weeks, the first Pay Day came. It was common practice at that time for the principal to hand paychecks directly to the teachers. This was a new teacher's first check and you had to know how much they looked forward to it.

Following is what happened with every new teacher. I would hand them their first ever check and a pen. I would then tell them in a matter of fact voice that they had to sign the back of the check and return it to me. If they hesitated and most did not, I would assure them that this was the practice and that they were probably told so at their interview. (Please don't get angry yet!)

I did this for years. Scores of teachers signed their name on the back and handed me their check. I would then look them in the eye and tell them that I was just a principal who was there to help them with their job and if they had any doubts about what was happening or what I said that they should feel free to question me. I went on to say in as light hearted a way as I could muster, "Here's your check back. You earned it. You would have been right to question me about my reason for taking your check. So from now on, I want you to feel free to question anything I do or say that you either disagree with or don't understand. But don't feel too foolish about giving me your check. All but one new teacher before you returned their signed check to me and he worked in a different district before coming to teach here."

They smiled and took their check back and I hoped they understood that I meant what I said. It was meant to break the ice that exists between teachers and principals and I think it often did. Fear was the last thing I wanted from the people who were delivering the service. Teaching is hard enough without worrying if you are pleasing the principal. I was there to help them do their job! A teacher and I would refer to the incident from time to time when it was appropriate and we would get a good laugh out of it.

The New Superintendent

Richard Jones had just been hired during the summer as our new Superintendent. We were briefly introduced to him at our first administrators meeting. He seemed like a nice guy who would be easy to work with but you never know.

The summer vacation was almost over. I was in my office taking care of the myriad of little details for getting the school ready to begin another school year. One of them was what to do with the money that was left over from our winnings and loses accumulated from the previous year's lottery wagers. Sixteen of us had formed a group that bought a lottery ticket each week hoping to win millions of dollars that we would share. There were many suggestions for what to do with the money but the one that won was that we each should bet $2.00 on a horse. We had enough money so that each person had $2.00 to bet. What does this have to do with Richard Jones you ask? You'll see.

The problem I was working on was selecting a horse on which to bet my $2.00. I was in the outer office pouring over that day's tout sheet when I sensed that someone was watching me. I looked up to see the new Superintendent standing on the other side of the counter looking at what was capturing my attention. How's that for a first impression?

He with a straight, serious face asked what I was doing looking at a tout sheet? He went on to say, "Is this what principals do in this town?" He was from Boston. I was flustered to say the least. I explained about the money left over from our New York State lottery winnings and in an effort to justify our action, how the money from the lottery was going into funding education. It really doesn't but that's another story. He listened, broke into a smile and reached into his pocket. He took out two dollars and asked if he could join the group. We both laughed out-loud. Neither of us forgot that first meeting. It helped both of us form an excellent working relationship. He broke the ice! PS. We all lost our $2.00!

Principals set the tone for their school, Superintendents for their district.

My Fifth Grade Student

Being the only experienced male teacher of the fifth grade, I would get the class that contained the grade's discipline problems. At the end of the year with a particularly difficult class, I asked my principal to, just once set me up with a class of the "Good Kids" for next year. He did!

Rather than having to be the disciplinarian all the time, I could just be their teacher. One minute I could kid with them and then in a minute I could get their attention and they would be ready the lesson. That did not eliminate challenges it just changed them.

This story is about one student among many. Susan was part of the class that was filled with outstanding fifth grade students. She was especially bright, intelligent, anxious to learn and a joy to teach. On the last day of that school year, I said goodbye to this wonderful class and watched them leave for the summer. Next year they would go on to the junior high school and I was left to wonder how they would progress?

Years passed and I was attending another high school graduation which I did each year. I would sit in the back of the auditorium and listen to the names of the students as they were called to the stage. Each name called was followed by a short description of their awards and plans for the future. When I recognized a name, I would listen very carefully.

On this particular evening, I was at the graduation of that wonderful class that I said goodbye to seven years earlier. Susan was part of the class that was graduating that evening. Her name was called followed by a list of very prestigious awards that she had achieved. How proud I was to hear how well she had continued to do! Then I heard her plans. She was going on to secretarial school. My joy turned to disappointment. She was so college material!

After all the names were called and the formal part of the evening was done I went up to Susan and was immediately recognized. I congratulated her on winning those wonderful awards. We spoke of the great 5th grade class we both enjoyed seven years earlier. Then I asked her why she was not going to college? She looked a little defensive and said, "Good secretaries are also needed in this world." "Of course" I agreed, "but going to college means you can be anything you want to be including a secretary." I must have looked a bit disappointed for her to say what she did. Later I was sorry for putting a damper on her special day.

I often thought about students who I had taught that were college material but never attended college. I realized then that students and parents decide long before high school about their children's attending college. Some decide even before they are born! That understanding gave me the ideas for creating the Good Scholarship Association and initiating a College Visitation Day for 5th grade students. Raising expectations and helping to plan for their future was a worthy effort. But that's another story.

About 20 plus years passed. I was standing near the front door of the school where I was the Principal. A beautiful, young woman approached me and introduced herself using her married name. She then went on to tell me that I knew her as Susan. Wow! How often had I thought of her and that graduation day? But what was she doing here at school? Was she registering a child? "No," she said, "I am substituting in your school."

In a flash, I realized that she somehow did go to college and become a teacher. I remembered her going for secretarial school and asked her about that. She proceeded to tell me that my disappointing words spoken to her at graduation stuck in her head. They rang in her head as they did in mine.

After marrying and raising her children, she began her college career and had just gotten her degree and license. Tears came to my eyes. I hugged her and told her that I would do everything I could to have her become a permanent teacher in my school.

As luck would have it, an opening came about a short time later and my wish came true. I introduced her to everyone as one of my best fifth grade students and now will be one of our best teachers.

Writing this has brought a smile to my face as I relived the many wonderful events we shared.

You never know what lasting effect your words might have.

Chapter 19

Genius Is Rare

The Egyptologist

During my 40 some years in education, I have come across many very bright students. Learning was easy for them and teaching them was a challenge for the teacher who had to keep them interested. In all my years, I have met only one true genius.

It was early in November when Mrs. Ryan, a Kindergarten teacher, brought one of her students to my office. She said she wanted me to meet this youngster named Charles. There before me was a cute little boy who was about as tall as the door handle. I love meeting new children but I also felt this was going to be special.

I stood, shook his hand and asked him why his teacher brought him to see me. He answered, "Because I'm an Egyptologist." These words coming out of this five-year old really got my attention. I smiled and, trying to keep a straight face, asked, "And what makes you an Egyptologist?" He starred back at me with a look of distain and said, "Because I know everything about Egypt." Being almost at a loss for words I said, "Well tell me something that you know about Egypt."

What followed was a very full description of King Tutankhamen, better known as "King Tut" The Boy King. I stood there listening to this little guy spout words that were bigger than him. He told me how Howard Carter discovered the Sarcophagus in 1922 and there was an exhibit at the British Museum. He was fascinated with the facts of Tutankhamen's birth in 1342 BC, how he became King in

1333 BC and when he died at the age of 19 in 1323 BC. This... coming from a five year-old!

All this time his index finger was pointed toward me and his head was bobbing up and down to emphasize his explanation. He not only could pronounce the words, he knew what they meant. I was very impressed and told him so.

The year was 1972 and King Tut was all over the media. That accounted for the interest Charles had with the subject. One thing was sure he certainly was a smart little guy. After school that day, I spoke to his teacher. She told me that he could read those words and that he understood what he read and could even spell them. Now I realized that he was very, very smart. I decided to get to know him better.

One day I happened to see him in the lunchroom and I sat down next to him. He showed no discomfort with me sitting next to him so I started asking him questions. I asked if he was interested in things other than, Egyptology? He told me he was even more interested in the cosmos. At that time Carl Sagan, the famous astronomer, was doing a weekly television program about "The Cosmos". Charles told me he would watch that program whenever he could. I wondered why he added the words, "Whenever I can." He told me there was only one TV in the house and sometimes his parents wanted to watch other programs that were on at the same time. That triggered an idea.

It so happened that I had a TV and a reel-to-reel tape recorder in my office provided by the local cable company. I told Charles that I would record the programs and we could watch it while having lunch together the day after it viewed. He loved the idea.

The first viewing day came and Charles carried his lunch tray into my office. We settled in and I started the tape. His eyes were glued to the television set. That particular segment had to do with

Centrifugal Force. At one point he turned to me and said, "Is that why when I am riding in the car and my father makes a sharp turn I'm pushed to the other side?" Wow! Understanding this concept was far beyond any 5 year-old I knew.

We watched the entire series together and Charles continued to amaze me with his ability to understand concepts that were far beyond his years. The question then became how could we provide a curriculum that would stimulate his interests. Kindergarten was fine because he was learning how to interact with other children but what could we do for his academics when he reached first grade? The district had no classes or even a program for gifted kindergarten children.

I met with his parents to discuss the situation. They told me that, "Charles is an only child". They realized that he was far above other children his age in intellect and he would need a great deal of special assistance. There was no special help around. They said, "Charles can be very hard to deal with at times." I could imagine!

At some point, it dawned on me that Charles was as far to the right of the IQ norm as TMR (<50 IQ) children are to the left. He was special and he needed different programming. How could we accommodate his needs? I suggested to his parents that they investigate a special school for the gifted for Charles. They dismissed that plan. We would have to do the best we could.

When Charles started first grade it was obvious that there was very little in the curriculum that he could not do or that interested him. He was bored and became a behavior problem for the teacher. He relished it when he had a challenging project to do. However, he kept asking questions that interrupted what the teacher was doing with the rest of the class. Too bad computers were not around then! While he could handle the more advanced material, his social skills were poor.

By the next grade, things got much worse. It was clear that the behavior problems Charles had were going to be disruptive to the class and his teacher. What could we do? Meantime, I found time to meet with him and had him do a project for me. I read an article about solving difficult problems and what it emphasized was to 'think outside the box'. That's what we had to do!

A thought came to me that was certainly outside the box. What if we could get Charles to a class that would challenge him? How about getting him to the junior high or senior high and allow him join in with a science class? I ruled out the junior high because I did not think that age group could handle this situation. That left the senior high school!

I called my fellow high school principal and friend, Paul O'Brien, and told him about Charles and the problem. I assured him that Charles was very special and could read and understand scientific concepts at a 10th grade level. I could hear him gulp when I got to the plan. The plan was for Charles to join a science class at the high school. I would see to the transportation needs and get the consent of all those who needed to know. What I needed from him was the name and the agreement of a teacher and a group of students who would get a kick out of this challenge.

He called back the next day. He simply said, "12th grade Earth Science. It's a regents class, only 14 students who were very nice and they all agreed to give it a try." But a 12th grade Regents class? Would this be too much for Charles? Well if it was too much we could always stop the plan.

I consulted with and got agreement from his parents, John at the bus garage, the assistant superintendent, his teachers and of course Charles. I think everyone was anxious about trying the plan except for Charles. He just wanted to get started.

Every day the bus would bring him to the high school for the one period and then bring him back to us. By the end of the second week we knew the plan was working. Charles was working hard to catch up to the class because he started six weeks after the semester began. The high school students took Charles on as their mascot. They got a big kick out of this little guy sitting in class whose feet dangled because they did not reach the floor. The first time he raised his hand and answered the question correctly, the class cheered. Charles went on to pass the Earth Science Regents! When he was in fourth grade he took Biology and in fifth grade he took Chemistry, passing both Regents Exams. Our school was a K-5 so Charles was off to the junior high in grade six.

Sequel: Many years later, I was telling some friends about Charles and what he was able to do when he was in Kindergarten and the high school plan we worked out for him. I told them how proud I was of the people who made the plan work and the district that made it possible. They were very impressed and asked me if I was still in touch with Charles? I said "No", but I was certainly interested in what became of the little guy who was now all grown up. They suggested that I "Google" him. What a great idea! I entered his name in the search box and received three biographies and a description for each.

One of the descriptions was obviously the correct one. His bio had an e-mail address. I e-mailed the following message: "Are you the same person who was brought to my office when you were in Kindergarten claiming to be an Egyptologist?" He e-mailed a response within days saying that he was that kid. We exchanged e-mails a few times. He told me what he was doing and I told him I was very proud of him.

When all else has failed, think outside the box.

Chapter 20

The Letter People & Making Decisions

The Best Kindergarten Program

This took place in the '60s, not to be confused with today.

If there was ever a wonderful method for teaching Kindergarten children how to read, it was with the Letter People. I do not remember the name of the person who came up with the idea but she really knew five-year old children. The Letter People Program was comprised of the 26 balloon-like letters of the alphabet. Each balloon was the size of the five year-olds who would learn to identify the names of the letters and the sounds they made.

They were colorful standup balloons imprinted with wonderful faces in crazy costumes that would capture the imagination of all. They were made of heavy plastic that could withstand much of the rough handling they would get from Kindergarten youngsters.,

All the consonants were male and all the vowels were female. Their names had to do with the sound their letter made. So… "Tall Teeth" represented the letter T and the balloon had elongated teeth. There was a book and a tape that played a catchy song for each letter. The Kindergarten teachers I knew loved the concept. The kids loved it even more than I did!

Everything was going along very well, until one day when the assistant superintendent, who initiated the program, came to see me. I could tell by the expression on his face that he was here for something serious. He proceeded to tell me of a junior high, female teacher was lodging a complaint relative to the fact that in the Letter

People Program the Consonants were all male and the Vowels were all female. She claimed this was sexist!

At first, I thought he was kidding. After he got into the details of the complaint I realized, he was telling it like it was. This woman, who was into the Feminist Movement, would look for any reason she could find that would create a feminist issue.

We talked about the complaint and I had a difficult time being serious. We finally decided to form a plan. My advice was for him to thank the woman for her input and then ignore the issue. The program was too good to let one person make it end. That brings me to the way I treated most complaints of this nature. Through the years, I have found that there are often people who are extremely negative toward any new issue. They speak the loudest while those who are either satisfied or even in favor of the issue remain silent.

With this in mind, I treated any criticism with respect but realized that others may think differently about the same issue. I tried to remind people who make decisions that a few negative, outspoken people do not necessarily speak for the majority. Too often, a vocal person or group would attend a Board meeting and get things changed to what they wanted at the expense of what was working well. My rule was to say, "I will think about your request and let you know my decision and thank you for bringing the matter to my attention." I must admit I did not always follow my rule and mostly regretted not having done so.

The assistant superintendent took my advice. Neither of us realized at that time how tenacious a person this complainer was. This woman would not go away! She rallied support from others and drafted a petition that ordered the secession of the program. She got a number of people to sign the petition and took it to the assistant superintendent. He became flustered. He showed me the petition that contained scores of signatures. I told him that probably half the signatories didn't even know what they were signing but that didn't help.

We looked at the signatures and the petition and considered how it should be answered. We decided to call the woman who had created the program. When we read the petition to her and told her how many people had signed it she said she had not heard of this complaint before. After some discussion, she came up with the best answer. She suggested we answer the petition by saying, "Vowels are in fact more important than Consonants to 5-year-olds." Tell those who signed the petition that every Consonant needs at least one Vowel to form a word. "So in fact, all Consonants are dependant on Vowels."

We settled this issue by sending a letter to each signatory saying that every one of our Kindergarten teachers would remind their kids how important Vowels were in the English language. As an administrator, you never know from where the next problem will come.

That's what makes the job so interesting.

Chapter 21

Teacher Observation

Best results

The Lesson

I always considered "dropping in" unannounced to observe a teacher to be very unprofessional. No other profession that I can think of would permit that. Yet, it is a common practice among educators. If the visit is meant to catch the teacher off guard, then you might be seeing that teacher at his or her worst. I want to see the best lesson that the teacher can give. That way the lesson can become a benchmark from which to measure future lessons. If the planned lesson is poor, then you know that something has to be done.

I have tried many ways to observe a teacher's lesson that would be helpful to the teacher and fulfill my supervisory obligations as a principal. I kept in mind that the purpose of supervision is to improve performance therefore it should be a collaborative experience. By that I mean both the teacher and the supervisor should plan the observation together with most of the planning coming from the teacher. There are many ways to make the experience satisfactory to both. Following is a formal observation I did with a first year, third grade teacher that both of us said really helped.

Miss M. and I had our pre-observation discussion to determine the topic of the lesson. She chose a lesson about weather that was part of the science curriculum. To make it more exciting she chose to include severe weather such as hurricanes, tornadoes and blizzards. I told her that sounded very interesting and I was looking forward to the lesson.

I asked her if there was a particular teaching skill that she wanted me to focus on. She said she needed help with her questioning techniques. I made a note of that and told her I would concentrate on that skill. Then I asked her to tell me the configuration of the students in the classroom. She said there were 24 students who would be sitting at six tables with four students at each table.

I explained that I would sit in an inconspicuous place in the room and would be writing for the entire time. We looked over the form together so she knew what I was doing. The form was on an 8x10 sheet of lined-paper. The first column, about an inch wide, contained the running time of the lesson. The remaining seven inches were divided in half with "Teacher's Action" written on the left side and "Students' Action" on the right side.

I explained that, "as the lesson progresses I will keep a record of the time. Next to it, I will write what you were doing at that time. Next to that, I will write what the students were doing. By the end of the lesson, I will have gathered a great deal of information. I will then thank you and the class and return to my office. You will get a copy of the completed form to look at before we set up our Post Observation discussion." She said that she understood the directions.

Before the observation, Miss M made a map of the room that indicated where each student would be sitting. I prepared an easy to use set of symbols to show what was going on at any specific time. For example, I used a + for a yes/no question. A ++ for a question that required a more complete answer and a +++ for an answer that led to a discussion. I used a * for a correct answer and an x for a wrong answer. Using these and other symbols I could quickly map what was going on and when it was happening. This method could be used to focus on discipline, timing and classroom management, modality or any other focus. The form would look something like this:

Time	Teacher's Action	Students' Action
000	Handing out ditto	Quietly getting ready
001	Opening question +	B4*
002	Have you experienced...	++A2* D1* B3*

When we got together for the post-observation discussion Miss M. already knew a great deal about the lesson. She was able to see who answered the questions and who did not. She could tell which of her questions were effective. In addition, she noted the pace of the lesson. She felt she spent too much time in one area and not enough time in another. At the conclusion of the discussion she said that seeing the lesson in this format gave her the opportunity to see for herself the areas that worked well and those that needed attention. I told her she did very well and I was sure she was on her way to becoming a Master Teacher.

Times Change, Methods Change

Wear a tie

John had taught music at the high school for a number of years. Due to declining enrollment, John was moved to my elementary school. In addition to teaching, he played in a rock band. He came to school looking the same way that he looked on weekends playing in the band including a large earring that dangled from his right ear. The kids loved him! He was one of them. The problem was that the students treated him as if he was one of them. When it came time for him to teach the lesson, he could not control the class. Teaching is very difficult for anyone who has to fight for control!

I observed John as he tried to teach a second grade class and it was very apparent that he could not get control of the class. The lesson went poorly. The kids were all over the place. He struggled to get them to listen and follow his directions, to no avail.

At our post observation conference, he looked exhausted. We spoke about the problems he had getting through the lesson. We looked at the results of the time line form I used for his observation. It was clear that the class was only able to remain on task for 12 of the 30 minutes. We talked about some of the things that were contributing to his problems. The one I focused on was that trying to talk over the noise made by the students caused him to speak louder and he had to shout instructions. That is very tiring and very ineffective! I made some recommendations.

Subsequent observations showed that he was not getting much better. Each time we agreed that he had to improve his basic control and each time he tried. The final test came when his chorus was required to put on a concert for parents and grandparents. He panicked! "What should I do, I can't get them to listen?"

He was ready for my real advice. There was a time when, what I was about to tell him would have been said in a very early discussion. Times had changed and I had to wait for the right time to say, "What I am about to tell you is beyond the scope for me as a principal to require of you. If you do not want to hear it, pay no attention. Your appearance is causing many of your problems. The kids love you but they do not respect you! You have it the other way around. For openers get a haircut, remove the earring, wear a white shirt, tie and jacket, tell the students to call you Mr. and always by your last name. I know that this cannot be required, but considering how you are struggling, you may want to try it."

Some rebuttal was expected, but instead he became very pensive and left the office. The next time I saw him his appearance had changed dramatically. He had made all the changes we had discussed. The only thing I had to do was teach him how to tie his tie. The change was almost immediate with the students. After a few weeks, there was a marked improvement in his lessons. He finally got the respect from the students that he needed to maintain control. Above all, he did not look exhausted at the end of the day.

Years went by and I saw John at a retirement dinner. There he was in a shirt, tie and jacket, no earring and a short haircut. He made it a point to come over to me and thank me for, "setting him straight".

You seldom know the lasting effect you have on a person's life. When you do, and it is positive, it is very rewarding.

Chapter 22

Praise vs. Punishment

The "Gotcha" Award

In keeping with reward and praise for doing good deeds, we started the "Gotcha" award. Any student or teacher who witnessed a person doing a good-deed could put that person in for a "Gotcha" award. The award was a 3x5 card titled "Gotcha" that included the recipient's name, and a description of the deed the person witnessed.

I would sign the award and call the recipient to my office. Upon their arrival, wondering what they had done, I would shake their hand and tell them who recommended them and what they did to deserve a "Gotcha" award. I would then thank them for the part they played in making our school a better place for everyone. This was followed up with a phone call to the proud parents.

The day the "Gotcha" awards started Brenda, a fifth grade girl, came to my office. She explained that her teacher had just told the class about the new program called "Gotcha" and she thought her best friend Tina deserved a "Gotcha".

I told her she would be the first but she had to tell me what Tina did to deserve a "Gotcha". She went on to tell me that she was very worried about a math test that was coming up the next day. She had been sick for the previous week and missed the lessons that would be on the test. She said, "I never failed a test in my whole life but I knew I would fail this one."

Tina called her that afternoon and said she knew how upset she must be about the test. If she would like she would come to her house and show her what she had missed. The impromptu tutoring session resulted in Brenda passing the test. It also resulted in giving Tina the first "Gotcha" award.

I gave out many "Gotcha" awards during the years that followed but none was as cute as the one I gave to a boy named Billy. James, a fellow Kindergartener, came to my office with his teacher who asked him to tell me why he thought Billy deserved a "Gotcha". James said, "Biwwy (James could not pronounce his "L"s yet) should get a "Gotcha" because he asked me to be his friend." He went on to say, "I didn't have any friends and Biwwy saw that every day I was standing 'awone' on the 'pwayground'. James came over to me and asked if I wanted to 'pway' with him. I said 'yes' and we became best friends."

His teacher told me that James was very shy and she and his mother were worried about him. What Billy had done that day made a significant difference in the way James felt about going to school. I do not know if any adult could have done for James what Billy did for him.

I absolutely agreed that Billy deserved a "Gotcha" for being so nice and helping a fellow classmate. James was very pleased that his friend was going to get a "Gotcha". The teacher and James returned to class and told Billy that he should go to the principal's office. He had no idea why he was going to the principal's office, Had he done something wrong?

James accompanied him to my office whereupon I shook his hand and handed him the "Gotcha" award. I read aloud from what I wrote on the 3x5 card. "To Billy. This "Gotcha" award is given to you for being so nice to a fellow classmate when you saw that he needed a friend".

I then called Billy's mother and told her about the "Gotcha" award I had just given her son. She could not have been happier.

Years went by and at their elementary school graduation, Billy's mother came over to me to show me what she was holding. It was the "Gotcha" award that I had given Billy six years ago. She had it framed and it hung in his room all these years.

More times than not the principal is called upon to reprimand and punish a misbehaving student. That's part of the job and is how it should be. The Principal of a school is the ultimate authority and as such has that responsibility.

Too often as a result, the principal has the reputation by the students of being, "mean". Many students who never get into trouble were fearful of the principal and never wanted to be, "Sent to the principal's office". The "Gotcha" award was meant to change that perception. When necessary, I could be stern in dealing with a misbehaving student, but I could also be friendly and happy to see the many "good" kids who attended our school.

Don't be afraid to smile... It makes you and others feel good!

Chapter 23

Praise When Deserved, Works Wonders

New Art Teacher

A few days before the school year began, Sharon Bloomfield, our new art teacher, came to the school to introduce herself and see her art room. I felt a little embarrassed about the paltry art supplies she would have to work with. The art budget always took second place to reading, math and the other academic subjects. So… I told Sharon how inventive her predecessor was and that, "she even made her own clothing." Do not ask me why I said that. Just looking at Sharon you knew she was not sewing her own clothing.

She was right out of college and raring to go. She was going to show me that even though she did not sew her own clothing she was going to be the best art teacher ever. I showed her the meager art supplies that we had in the store room half expecting her to be critical. She looked but said nothing. Instead, she set to work finding ways to use low or no cost material in order to turn them into works of art.

In a few weeks, the walls of the building were brimming with the children's art. Everybody noticed including me! I told her how teachers and parents were commenting on how beautiful the building looked since she became our art teacher. She loved the accolades and set out to do even more just to prove that she was worthy of them. That got her even more praise and then there was no stopping her.

One of her greatest achievements was her end of the year art show. It was the culmination of a year's worth of imagination, talent and her wonderful way with the students. Under her direction, the children became our interior decorators. They felt proud of the way their school looked and they did a lot to keep it that way. Graffiti became nonexistent.

Not only had they learned to produce art they discovered how to appreciate it. Sharon found a very inexpensive collection of art prints that could form the beginnings of an art museum within the school. Students would learn about the masters and recognize their work. The prints were cheap but the frames cost a fortune. Sharon solved the problem. She got the PTA to buy wooden slats. Then she got Ben, our head custodian, to make the frames. When the frames were finished, she painted them, mounted the prints and hung them in our newly created art museum wing. Sharon's personality was such that you could not say "no" to her. She reminded me of the story of "Stone Soup".

The story is about a soldier on his way home after the war. He was very hungry but had no money to buy food. He came to a town and the people seeing him hid. They knew that soldiers would be asking for food and they did not want to part with any of theirs. But this soldier was different. All he asked for was a pot filled with water and a stone so he could make "Stone Soup". The towns-people were very interested in how he could make this soup that cost nothing, so they gave him a pot filled with water. He placed the pot on the stove, found a large stone that he put in the pot and started cooking. The towns-people were fascinated.

As the water was about to boil he said, "This soup would be even better if it had a bit of parsley in it." That was cheap enough, so someone gave him some parsley. Next, he said the soup would be even better with a carrot then a potato then some celery and finally "a little piece of meat". You get the idea. This is how Sharon got more than her share of the school's budget. In the end her "soup" tasted great!

As the years went by Sharon's ideas and her end of the year art show grew to memorable proportions. Each student's artwork was displayed for all to see. Parents flocked to the annual art show and their praises filled the halls. The more she was praised the greater became her art show until the local fire department finally objected. But that's another story.

Give Them All an 'A'

This same art teacher came to my office with a problem. She was required to enter a grade for art on each student's report card. That had been the practice for all the years. She had a problem with what criteria to use for the grade. Should it be the quality of the work or the effort shown or how they behaved in class? What does an A mean and what does a D mean? We pondered these questions and then she came up with the idea that was lurking in the back of her mind. How about giving each student an A for their grade in art?

Would that diminish the importance of art? How would the students and their parents react to this? Art teachers were required to give a grade in art but nothing in the rules said what the grade must be. She was so convincing that I said, "Let's try it and see what happens."

The classroom teachers agreed with the idea but not many of the other art teachers in the district did. They felt that it would "diminish" the importance of Art. I wondered if they sometimes used the grade as a threat regarding student behavior? They also felt that the students would not work as hard if they knew they would get an A no matter what they did. In spite of their concerns, we decided to try it.

The Results:

The kids loved seeing an A on their report card. For some it was the first A they had ever seen. We heard that the going rate for each A was $1 so it stimulated the economy. The best was that the students worked even harder to get another A on their next report card. In no way did it diminish their effort or behavior. In fact, both improved.

To my knowledge, Sharon continues to give each of her students an A on their report card. Once again, praise and the receiving of an A, got better results than an F got, used for punishment!

If you want teachers to be professional, treat them professionally.

Chapter 24

When In Doubt, Try Humor

Free Jessica Tate:

The parents of a child in our special education program were unhappy with the results of a psychological test that Pete, our psychologist had administered. In a switch of roles, the parents thought the child was more disabled than his tests had indicated and the teacher's input showed. The disagreement went back and forth for a while until they took their son to a private clinic for testing. I do not know what they told the people there about us but it caused them to send us a rather nasty letter explaining the legal rights of their client. We on the other hand felt that we were acting in the best interest of the child and that further intervention would do more harm than good.

After additional back and forth discussion that was getting us nowhere, Pete and I decided the best way was to talk to the people at the clinic face to face. We made an appointment to meet with them at their office. We realized that all three parties involved were concerned for the child's welfare, but we needed to reach agreement on how to serve his interests best. Confrontation was not furthering the cause.

During this time, a television program called "Soap" was airing weekly. It was a comedic spoof! Jessica Tate, the main character had been falsely convicted of murdering her tennis pro. We, the audience knew it was not true but what could we do? With tongue in cheek, we made large buttons saying "Free Jessica Tate". Anyone who watched the program would know what the phrase stood for. Pete and I each wore a button to the meeting.

Upon our arrival, we were ushered into the psychologist's office by her stone-faced secretary. The psychologist too looked very serious until she saw the buttons containing the words "Free Jessica Tate".

Fortunately, she was a serious devotee of the program. When she saw the button, she laughed out-loud! We spent the next ten minutes sharing portions of the program that brought guffaws of laughter to all of us. I removed my button and handed it to her. The ice was broken and the rest of the meeting was very productive. We both realized that we were interested in the well being of the student. We agreed on modifications that would better serve the child. Their psychologist offered to call the parents and explain the new plan. Humor saved the day and benefited the youngster.

Andrew Drev*******

The principal has many roles. One of the most important is that of the school's ultimate disciplinarian. When a teacher has exhausted every means for getting an unruly student to behave in an appropriate manner, she or he should feel free to send that child to the principal's office. The principal, in turn, should make it clear that the misbehaviors would not be tolerated.

One morning, soon after I became the Principal, that lesson was thrust upon me. One of my outstanding first grade teachers came to my office and told me she wanted me to give two of her boys a tongue lashing for fooling around in class and not getting their work done. These were six-year-old children! I could be and had been very stern with fifth graders but first graders? I didn't feel up to it! She insisted that as the Principal this was one of my roles. I tried to avoid the issue but she insisted. Finally, I called her and said she could send the boys to my office.

I spent the few minutes it took for them to reach my office trying to get myself into a serious mode and wondering how I would approach the assignment. My secretary buzzed the intercom to tell me that the two boys were in the outer office. "Send them in!" I said in a loud, stern voice that was meant for the boys to hear.

Two little boys, fighting back tears, stood before me. One had blond hair and blue eyes. His chin was quivering. The other was a redhead with freckles across the bridge of his nose. How could I do this? Was this really what a principal had to do? Okay! For some reason, I chose to start with the kid with the quivering chin.

I picked up a pad and pencil and, trying to sustain my authority stature, asked in a most serious tone, "What's your name?" With my pencil poised and my eyes looking down at my pad, I waited for his answer. It came in a frightened voice, "Andrew." I wrote "A N D R E W" on my pad. I still didn't know where I was going with this so I asked for his last name. He said something that I could not understand so I told him to spell it. He said, in a high-pitched voice, "I can't!"

Now I had something to work with! I looked him right in the eye and said, "See, if you had been paying attention in your class instead of fooling around you would have learned how to spell your own name by now." I felt a little better with the direction this was taking.

With a show of authority, I buzzed Barbara my secretary. When she answered, I asked her to tell me how to spell Andrew's last name. She came to the door with a 3x5 card and began to read from it:

Barbara, reading from the card, "D r e v"

Me writing, D-r-e-v

Barbara reading, "a t"

Me writing, a t

Barbara reading, "o l"

Me: writing, o l (Me thinking 'How long can this go on?')

Barbara continuing to read, "i t"

Me: I began to lose it. How could I have asked this little guy to spell this name? But I pressed on, i t

Barbara, "s c h"

I lost it! I couldn't even pronounce it let alone spell it! I looked up at this chin-quivering little guy and said, "Andrew, if you know how to spell your name by the 5th grade it will be okay" and I sent them back to class. I never spoke to the other boy whose name was Steven Pebler. If I chose him first, I would never have had this story.

Sequel:

Years later, sitting in the back of the auditorium at a high school graduation, a tall, handsome, blond young man came over to me and said,

"D r e v a t o l i t s c h" It was Andrew. We both laughed out loud!

Chapter 25

Innovations That Work

Setting Up Next Year's Classes

It did not take me very long as Principal to know that I could avoid many problems for the coming year by carefully setting up the following year's classes. The reading teacher and some classroom teachers met with me and created a 3x5 card that looked like this:

Student's name_____

Teacher's name_____

Suggested reading group_____

Deportment (Circle)   A   B   C   D   F

Separate from_____

Join with_____

Special needs (speech, ESL, reading)_____

Teacher preference_____

At the end of May, teachers filled out their 3x5 cards and gave them to the reading teacher. She and I would temporarily make up the classes for the following year. We considered all the information gleaned from the 3x5 cards in order to make sure the classes were evenly balanced as to number, sex, ability and deportment.

When completed the new-class cards were returned to the current teachers. They would review each class to see if we had overlooked any problems and bring them to our attention. When each teacher agreed that we had considered and correctly set up the classes for the following year, we sent the cards to the following year's teachers for any last minute changes.

After all concerns were met, the cards were given to the secretary who typed the class lists. Finally the lists were returned to the teachers who would enter the name of next year's teacher on the student's report card. It took time but it was time well spent.

One more thing: Parental requests for their child having a particular teacher would be considered and if the child fit the criterion for that class it would be honored. There were never very many,

Time used for the prevention of problems is time worth spending!

High Interest Groups for the Winter Doldrums

As a fifth grade teacher I often felt that Friday afternoons, particularly during winter's fowl weather, were used as, "get ready time" for the weekend. Many considered it a waste of time. It was not a time to begin something new or review something just completed.

When I became a principal, I thought about making Friday afternoon a special time. I approached the 4, fifth grade teachers with the following idea; "What do you think about getting all the people, including those who have no classroom responsibility, to teach small groups of 5th graders on Friday afternoons during this winter? They could choose to teach anything in which they had a personal interest." They all thought the idea was worth pursuing.

I approached the art teacher, the music teacher, the two coaches, the librarian, the cook, the custodian, the school psychologist and the two secretaries with the idea. The plan was for each to conduct four lessons on successive Fridays. Each lesson had to be something they liked to do, like a hobby or a skill. Counting me, there was the potential for 15 people being involved. There were about 100 students in the four classes so each group would be comprised of no more than seven students.

Every one of the people mentioned liked the idea and agreed to come up with four lesson plans. The lessons had to be unlike anything that was part of the curriculum. The cook chose to teach her group how to bake a cake and make cookies. The custodian would have his group make a jewelry box. The music teacher bought kazoos and had his group write original songs. The librarian had her students write their own biography. One of the secretaries wrote and put on a play. The psychologist taught checkers. My secretary said she would teach typing. I chose chess.

We all started to work on the details of our plan. When the plans were completed, the students chose three from the list that they would like to learn. As it turned out, we were able to place everyone into one of their three choices.

The first Friday afternoon was scheduled and the program started. I don't know who was more excited, the teachers or the students. The four sessions went as smoothly as could be. The small group that met with their new teacher got right into the project they chose. It was special!

After the four Friday sessions ended, the 15 of us met to discuss everyone's thoughts. All asked to do it again. We did two more Friday segments that took us through the winter doldrums. The students chose different topics for each segment. The best part was the non-teaching staff's experience with teaching. They loved it!

Turning Doldrums into Euphoria is a good thing!

Pencils: Inexpensive & Effective

One of the best investments I made with my discretionary funds was to purchase a large quantity of #2 pencils. The pencils were a dark blue with the name of the school, John F. Kennedy, written in gold. I found a myriad of reasons to give them out to deserving people. Originally, I only thought about giving them to students. They were always far more impressed with them than what they cost.

One day, a teacher I was praising asked if she was going to get a, "JFK pencil?" "Of course!" I said. That began my giving pencils to teachers for their outstanding work. PTA volunteers and some parents also got one for their service to the school. It had the same positive affect on adults as it did on children. JFK pencils became the trademark of praise for the school.

Getting Notices Read

The president of the PTA asked me to contribute a letter to the bulletin they sent home each month. I was happy to comply but wondered how many would get home and how many would be read by the parents. After I had contributed a number of articles, I decided to find out.

At the end of a particular article, I added a note saying that if a parent signed this notice and had their child return the bottom portion to me, I would reward the child with a JFK pencil. The next day a few students came to my office with the signed document and I gave them a pencil. The following day more youngsters came looking for their pencil. By the end of the week, scores of students were in line waiting for their reward. I thought the parents were actually looking forward to reading my letter. I found out that kids asked other kids how they got a pencil. When they learned what it took, they rushed home and got the PTA article read and signed.

So… if you want to be sure that a notice gets home, involve students and make getting it home worth their while.

A Note from the Principal in Their Report Card

As the Principal of an elementary school, I was often called upon to reprimand an unruly, disruptive student. I knew that if a teacher sent a youngster to me, it was for a good reason.

Although I didn't like doing it, I became very good at it. I knew just the right words to use, how strong I needed to make my voice and what the scowl on my face should look like. I also made it a practice to connect, in a positive way, with these youngsters in the days following the occurrence. I wanted them to know, that after the reprimand, the incident was over.

I realized however, that I was not getting to know the, "Good" students. The students who paid attention, did their work and were a pleasure to have in class did not get to see the principal. I was rewarding negative behavior and ignoring positive behavior. I decided to correct that.

I always read every student's report card before it was sent home. I looked at the grades and comments they received. I wanted a way to praise the students who were doing well. I tried to remember their names but I could not put a face to their name.

The idea came to me to write a congratulatory note to each student who received a good report card. I had scads of 4x6 note pads saying, "From the Desk Of" at the top. I wrote a note to each student who received an "A" in at least half of their subjects. I also wrote a note to those who showed a marked improvement. I asked their teachers to send those students to my office but not to tell them the reason.

These youngsters were not used to being summoned to the principal's office and I could see that some were confused and a little concerned. When I handed them their note, smiled and shook their hand, their concerned looks turned to broad smiles. They told me they could not wait to see the look on their parent's face when they told them they had to see the principal and then showed them the note that would be attached to their report card. I was finally able to get to know the wonderful students I seldom saw.

As years went by, students with good report cards knew they were going to be summoned to the principal's office. They no longer looked concerned as they walked into my office. They and I looked forward to the day. I received more praise and recognition from parents for this action than any other thing I ever did! In my assignments as mentor to new principals, I told them this was the best public relations thing I ever did and implored them to follow suit.

A fellow principal added to my written notes by giving me his great idea! "Why wait until report card time to recognize a student's good behavior?" He would enter a classroom carrying his cell phone. When he saw a student doing excellent work he would call that child's home. Can you imagine how the parent felt when she realized the Principal was calling to praise her child?

One day, many years later, I was speaking to a parent that had been a student in our school and was registering her child for Kindergarten. As we spoke, she opened her purse and took out a bunch of 4x6 sheets of paper that contained notes that I had written to her for her excellent report cards. She told me that her mother cherished them and gave them to her when her first child was born. She asked if I still wrote notes to children for their schoolwork. "Of course" I said.

What a good feeling we both shared!

The Best Teaching Tool since Chalk

8K

The year was 1984. I was the Assistant Superintendent in charge of Curriculum for the entire district. One day a salesman came to my office to tell me about a new machine that was going to revolutionize the world and teaching. He was carrying a "Commodore Pet". It was designed to be the first computer to be used in the classroom and it was loaded with 8 K of memory.

"What is a K?" I asked. He responded with words like bits, bytes, programming, and many others that were new to me but very interesting. I was very impressed and ready to learn more about this teaching tool that was going to change the classroom. The more I heard, the more I saw the possibilities grow for using this teaching tool. Little did I know then how right I was going to be!

I set up meetings with principals and teachers and had him return to demonstrate his "Pet" for them. They were as impressed as I was.

I was about to recommend buying these wondrous 8K machines when I had the good fortune to speak with a friend who was in the business of developing computers. He talked to me about what was just around the corner with regard to computers and that I should lease them rather than buy them.

I met with the Board of Education and explained what I had learned about bits, bytes, and the '8K Commodore Pet'. They too were impressed! Then I recommended leasing rather than buying a number of them. Many of the board members questioned that strategy, asking what we would have after the year when we had to return the machines. My one word answer was "Knowledge!" Knowledge is the bottom line product of education. Unlike manufacturers that produce something you can hold in your hand, we produce knowledge that remains in your brain.

They agreed, and we leased a number of 8K Commodore Pets. Teachers and students tinkered with them. By trial and error, they learned about what this new machine could do. For example, we learned that it took only 4K to land the LEM on the moon.

The following year Commodore came out with the "Commodore 64". It had, as the name suggests, 64K. This was too much for the Board to pass up and over my recommendation to lease the 64s they purchased a number of them. Note: The thumb sized flash drive used to store what I have written in this book contains 4 GIGs. The rest is history!

The revolution was underway.

Chapter 26

The Tough Decisions

Billy Stratford

Principals are sometimes called upon to make decisions that are "life changing". Those are always the most difficult! Many decisions are made and forgotten but some are remembered forever. The story of Billy Stratford is certainly one of these. Billy's mother and sister brought him to school one day to register for Kindergarten. However, this was not an ordinary Kindergarten registrant. Billy was profoundly deaf. At the age of four, exactly one year before, he contracted Spinal Meningitis and lost total hearing in both ears.

Mrs. S. was trying to raise Billy in as close to a normal life as possible. She told me that Billy had actually taught himself how to lip read in the year since he had become deaf. She wanted him to attend a regular school and asked me to evaluate him and decide what would be the best placement for him. I had no experience to go on. None! I told her that we would get the best advice from people who work with deaf children. Note: This took place in the 1960s, long before the handicap rules came about and before the deaf were referred to as "hearing challenged".

Our local BOCES expert was brought in to do the evaluations. They sent a wonderful person who did a full evaluation of Billy. Afterward we spoke. She was very impressed with Billy's spirit. "He is one tough little guy," she said. "He may be right for a try at a regular Kindergarten."

Billy was and is very special. He had a most indomitable spirit. Nothing could make him give up or quit. He would conquer frustration after frustration. His smile and spirit won everyone over. We all wanted him to succeed. "The Decision" was made. We would start Billy in our regular Kindergarten.

At the time, our Kindergarten students only met for a half-day. We set up a team meeting with the teacher from BOCES, the Kindergarten teachers, the nurse, all the special teachers and people who might have contact with him. Every last one said that they were anxious to try it. We decided to make an exception and have Billy attend both the morning and afternoon Kindergarten with the same teacher. That teacher was Mary Ellen Ryan. Mary Ellen was perfect for the task. She was the consummate Kindergarten teacher with all the attributes you would want. Billy's parents were kept in the loop and were pleased with the decision.

When school began that September, we all held our breath waiting to see if our decision was the right one or would the school for the deaf be better for him. We were prepared to make that move if and when it became obvious that he was not making progress in a regular class.

The first few weeks were difficult as we all learned how to communicate with Billy. The special teacher sent by BOCES helped him and the rest of us with lip reading. This was not easy but as the days passed, I could see that the teachers adjusted to Billy and he was adjusting to his new environment. We all thought "It was working" and it was.

The first year went by and we once again evaluated Billy's progress and the 'Decision'. Continue on to our first grade or send him to the school for the deaf? After much discussion with the first grade teachers who were added to the original group, and with their approval, we agreed to stay the course. That year saw Billy making slow progress in his academics but good progress in his social relationships.

The question at the end of first grade was the same as that at the completion of Kindergarten. After much discussion, the 'Decision' was made to move him to our second grade. His teacher was hand picked. Who would be best for Billy and whom would Billy be best for? Lynn Schiavone was selected. Lynn was an experienced teacher who was serious about teaching the basics of learning to her class. She accepted the challenge.

After a few weeks of the first semester, Lynn came to my office to discuss some doubts she had about the 'Decision'. As the work became more complex, Billy was falling further behind in his studies. Were our expectations for Billy too high? Maybe! But would he be better off in a school for the deaf? Once again, we would question the 'Decision'.

We decided to visit the school for the deaf and see how other deaf children were doing compared to Billy. We consulted the Principal of The Mill Neck School for the Deaf and explained our problem. She invited us to the school to see and evaluate it for ourselves.

Lynn and I journeyed to the school. It had been an estate before being turned into the school. The grounds and the school were beautiful! The Principal took us around to show us the up-to-date equipment they were using. She told us that they teach both sign language and lip reading to all their students. Class size was small and the students were receiving a lot of individual attention. We started to wonder about the 'Decision'.

We visited a second grade and looked at what the youngsters were doing. Surprisingly, Billy was at least equal to them academically. We walked around this beautiful facility, talked about the pros and cons and gathered information as we went. The Principal invited us to stay for lunch and we accepted.

The lunchroom, like the rest of the school, was beautiful. The children were at round tables for eight and the food looked great. But one thing was missing: sound! All that was heard were forks hitting plates. All the students were signing and not a word passed through their lips. Lynn and I looked at each other and had the same thought. Billy was living and progressing in the hearing world that our school could provide. The 'Decision' was made that we would keep him.

Billy continued his education all the way to high school graduation. He had his difficulties but he made it through. I monitored his progress through all the grades and we had a wonderful relationship. For many years after his graduation, Billy would come to see me. He knew how interested I was in his life. We would talk about what he was doing. His great smile and winning personality was certainly working very well for him. He studied auto mechanics and could tune a car's engine by feeling its vibrations. He loved to tell me about his love life which was always with hearing girls.

One day Billy came to my office and very excitedly asked me to see his new, rebuilt car. I followed him outside and there it was. He invited me to see the inside. Once inside he turned on the car radio. He had speakers all around the car. I was admiring the sound when it dawned on me that Billy could not hear any of it. I asked him why he put all the sound equipment into the car. His response said it all. "The girls love it!"

Billy lives in the hearing world. Last I heard he was engaged to a "hearing" girl. His friends are all "hearing" people. I once asked Billy about the 'Decision'. He said the people he knew that went to the school for the deaf hung around together and not with people who could hear. He was glad to live among the hearing world.

Don't Carry The Donkey

As a leader and a Principal, you will be called upon to make many decisions. Those who you lead will expect you to show them the way. So follow some basic rules about getting the information that will help you decide which way to go and then go!

I knew a principal who would be swayed from one decision to another by people who continued to offer advice after his decision was announced. He would try to please everyone so the last person to get his ear would become his final decision. Teachers would leave after a meeting with a direction to follow, only to find out that things had changed and the work they did would have to be redone.

Indecision causes anxiety and will eventually erode the ability to lead. A wrong decision can be corrected but indecision frustrates and goes on too long.

New PTA presidents are particularly vulnerable to this. They often feel that they must please everyone and wind up pleasing no one. In order to teach this lesson to my new PTA presidents and others, I would tell them the story called "The Man, The Boy and The Donkey." It comes from Aesop's Fables written in the 17th century and still is good advice today.

The Man, the Boy and the Donkey

A Man and his son were once going with their Donkey to market. As they were walking along by its side a countryman passed them and said: "You fools, what is a Donkey for but to ride upon?" So the Man put the Boy on the Donkey and they went on their way. But soon they passed a group of men, one of whom said: "See that lazy youngster, he lets his father walk while he rides." So the Man ordered his Boy to get off, and got on himself. But they hadn't gone far when they passed two women, one of whom said to the other: "Shame on that lazy lout to let his poor little son trudge along." Well, the Man didn't know what to do, but at last he took his Boy up beside him on the Donkey. By this time they had come to the town, and the passers-by began to jeer and point at them. The Man stopped and asked what they were scoffing at. The men said: "Aren't you ashamed of yourself for overloading that poor donkey of yours with you and your hulking son?" The Man and Boy got off and tried to think what to do. They thought and they thought, until at last they cut down a pole, tied the donkey's feet to it, and they carried the Donkey!

Don't find yourself carrying the donkey! In an effort to please all, we often please none!

Some Donkeys Need To Be Carried By the Principal

Mr. G

I became the Principal of the newly erected John F. Kennedy Elementary School as a result of a very fortuitous situation for me. It was not so for the assistant superintendent who had committed a felony that summer and was sent off to prison. The Principal of the newly built JFK School was elevated to Assistant Superintendent and I took her place as Principal of the brand new school. I began the job at the start of the second semester of the school's first year.

To say the least, I was very excited about my new assignment. The school was brand new and the staff had been hand picked by the now Assistant Superintendent for Curriculum who was my immediate boss. What could be better than that?

Even though I had worked in the district, I did not know any of the teachers or staff of the new school. I taught on the north end of the district and JFK was on the south end. The first thing that occurred to me was that the job was far different than I had expected. Whenever the principal of the school where I taught before would plan to be absent, he would ask me to take his place in "the

Principal's office". He was grooming me for an administrative position. As a result, I was convinced that I had enough experience to do the job. But when I went from agreeing with or judging the principal's decisions to the one being agreed with or judged, I realized how different it was going to be.

One of my first goals was to get to know the names of the teachers, the students and the staff. I used every opportunity to get to know the people with whom I was working. I stood at the front door every morning and greeted teachers and students as they entered the building. I smiled and practiced greeting them by name whenever I could.

One morning, only a few weeks into the job, I greeted a fourth grade teacher and thought I smelled alcohol on his breath. Could it be? Nah! I must be mistaken but I made sure to find a way to check his breath frequently. After a few days, I was convinced that he was drinking before coming to school or the odor of alcohol was left over from his heavy drinking the night before. In any case, I had to see if it was affecting his teaching.

During the next few weeks, I found reasons to get into his classroom even for a few minutes to see what was happening. There were days when he was fine but on many, his eyes were glazed and his speech was slurred. One day I found him sitting at his desk with his eyes closed. He was asleep. Often the kids did whatever they wanted as he sat at his desk. Day by day, I became more convinced that he was drinking and coming to school unable to function properly. His students were my concern! I knew that this was going to be my first serious problem but it needed to be resolved.

I looked at his personnel file. He had taught for many years and was tenured. My boss was his Principal for all those years. I read all the evaluations. They were all good to excellent. Now what? Was I way off base? After all, she was his boss for all those years. She observed his teaching and wrote those favorable reports that I found in his folder.

I decided to ask for a meeting with my new boss under the guise of her being able to familiarize me with the staff. So as not to single out my problem teacher, I began asking first about the Kindergarten teachers. One by one, she told me the strengths and weaknesses of the staff. I worked through the grades until I finally came to the fourth grade. I casually mentioned Mr. G's name, expecting some of my suspicions to come out. None were forthcoming. In fact, the report was fairly glowing. We continued on through the rest of the staff but I hardly could pay attention to her answers. My thoughts were on the problem. Either she never noticed the problem in all those years or she was covering up for her old friend. Here was the new Principal finding a problem in a matter of weeks. In either case how was I to approach the situation? I decided to say it up front and see her reaction.

When I told her what I had discovered she was shocked! After making sure that I was sure, she said we had to talk to the Superintendent. We made an appointment that day and I related what I found. He said, "Check his desk. If he's drinking he'll have it in his classroom." Check his desk? Was that legal? I was surprised by his comment but he was the boss and I was brand new.

That afternoon, after everyone had left the building, I checked his desk. Sure enough, there was a jar half filled with a clear liquid. I opened the jar and it was unmistakably alcohol. I called the Superintendent and told him how impressed I was and that he was right.

Mr. G was tenured which meant that he could not be summarily fired. I had to build a case and follow the procedures laid out by the law. But first, I had to know the law. The assistant superintendent and I met with the district's lawyer to go over the correct procedure that I was to follow. I knew this would be difficult but it needed to be done.

I set up a formal observation with Mr. G. He appeared very nervous during the pre-conference meeting. He wanted to know why he was chosen to be the first to have a formal lesson observation. I assured him that someone had to be first.

The day came and he had obviously fortified himself with alcohol. His speech was slurred and his eyes were glazed. He had difficulty staying on task and showed other signs of a lack of control. His lesson was poorly presented. Many of the issues we discussed during the pre-observation conference were left out. Learning was not taking place in this classroom!

Our post-conference was scheduled for that afternoon. When he entered the office, I noticed he was visibly shaken. I felt very sorry for him but I felt more sorry for the students who were being short-changed. He apologized and said he realized that the lesson went poorly. He was a good person with a serious problem and I was the one who had to confront him. My exact words at our post-conference were, "You and I know that you have a serious drinking problem."

At first, he denied it but after some discussion, he began to relax. It was as if he could finally unburden himself from this secret he had to keep for all this time. He told me that he was trying to deal with his drinking problems but they were overwhelming him. Having to hide it from a new Principal was going to be too difficult for him. We spoke about various options open to him, none of which included his continuing to teach. He chose to take an extended leave of absence until he could resolve his problem. We all agreed that was the best solution for all concerned. He never returned.

What followed was something I cannot forget. I sensed a coolness that came over many of the teachers in the building but I chalked that up to my being new to the school. It was not until many months had elapsed that a teacher told me what had chilled the staff. From their point of view, this new Principal came into the new job and the first thing he did was to get a long-time, tenured, fellow teacher to leave. It shook many of the teachers who had no idea of the facts of the situation. To make matters more difficult, I could not reveal the facts to the staff. I just had to work harder to get them rid of their fears and win the respect of the staff

Mrs. F

As standardized testing proliferates and passing the test becomes the measure of success or failure, new ways of preparing students for passing the tests become the norm. Most of these methods are legal, some are shady and some are totally illegal. As the emphasis on test scores increase, so does the shady and totally illegal methods that are used by some intimidated teachers. The more talk about Merit Pay and schools being closed based on the results of a test score, the more pressure will be placed on teachers to pass that one standardized test that determines pass or fail for the year.

After two years, I left the Assistant Superintendent's position and returned to being the Principal of an elementary school. My new assignment was in a school on the north side of the district. The building, staff and students were new to me. It was like starting over but this time with a good deal more experience. Once again, I was anxious to learn the names of the staff and students.

I set about getting to know the strengths and weaknesses of the teaching staff. The staff was fairly typical with many that were very good, some fair and one or two that needed some help but all anxious to do a good job.

After observing the teachers and looking at past test score results I noticed that one of the teachers whom I felt needed a good deal of help was in fact getting the best results in the standardized test scores. How could that be? The other teachers in her same grade level seemed to be better teachers yet their scores were lower than hers were. They figured that she was cheating and that their lower scores were making them look bad. Nevertheless, they could not accuse her outright. They would just raise their eyebrows whenever speaking of her success. I too suspected that she was using questionable methods to get these results, but how was she doing it and could I prove it?

When test week came around, I was determined to find how she was getting the test results that her class was scoring. I waited until after the first day's testing session. At the end of the day, I went to her room to look at the test booklets to see the results of this first session. The booklets were nowhere to be found. She had taken the booklets home. That was not permitted. The next morning I told her that the test booklets were never to leave the building. She looked upset but agreed to not doing that again.

I checked the booklets again after the second day and there was the answer. To make a long story short, it was plain to see that she simply took the test booklets home, a no-no, erased the wrong answers and replaced them with the correct answers. The erased answers were plain to see. When confronted with the evidence she broke down and said she was doing it to make the kids feel better about themselves. She was eligible to retire so we didn't have to go through legal procedures to get her dismissed. She voluntarily took her retirement.

The damage to the students was that their excellent test scores gave them a false sense of accomplishment. Their next year's teachers would soon find out that their test scores were inflated. But even more importantly, the other teachers on her grade level were presented with the problem of the consequences of their not cheating. When you know that you are competing with someone who is cheating, does that make you think about doing the same? That should never enter any teacher's mind! This was an extreme case but I wonder how many teachers, feeling the pressures, are finding "creative" ways to improve scores?

Beware the concomitants of judging teachers and schools based solely on Standardized Tests!

Chapter 27

Homework

By Prescription

"Homework"! The very word can send chills through the body of parents and students alike. It is one of the most controversial topics discussed by students, parents and educators. Many kids hate it and some parents hate it even more. "It takes away from my free time." "It cuts into my preparing dinner." "I have to badger my kid to finish." "Some kids love it." "It reinforces the day's work." "Research agrees that it produces a better learner." You can add any of the complaints and praises you have heard about.

So why should something that most agree does some good be bad-mouthed by so many? The answer I think is that not all homework is the same. That is to say, there is often too much that is given and some of it is just busy work. Some teachers give the homework assignment out early with instructions for students to start their homework during the period or day in order to give them something to do when they finish their work ahead of the others. Should that be called "homework"? Parents who would like to help often are frustrated because they do not know how!

That brings me to "Homework by Prescription".

Homework should be dispensed the way a doctor dispenses medicine. The medicine is specific to the illness; it is meant to cure and it contains directions for how it is to be taken. When there is no longer any illness, we discontinue taking the medicine. Homework assignments should follow the same concept!

Some rules that I followed:

Not every student needs to practice the same thing. Those who appear to know the material can use the time for some other more productive study.

Homework should be for practicing what was taught that day to reinforce learning the new concept. It is important that the student practice the material correctly. Practice does not make perfect. Perfect practice makes perfect! The student must know they are practicing the correct way.

Time limits must be established and should be followed by both teachers and parents. If you follow the ten minutes times the grade level rule, then a fifth grader should have no more than fifty minutes of homework. The parent should know that at the end of fifty minutes the student should stop even if they are not finished. The fact that a student could not finish the assignment can tell the teacher a lot about the assignment. It may be that the assignment was too long. It may mean this student needs more instruction for the assignment. It may mean this assignment was just right for this student.

Last but not least. All homework assignments should be reviewed by the teacher and returned to the student with a comment. If it's worth assigning it is worth checking. Kids soon know when homework is not checked and the results show it.

My own children are a good example for what I have said. My daughter loved to do homework. It was easy for her and it was like playing school for her. She wanted to be a teacher from the first time she was asked what she wanted to be. The schoolwork came easy for her and she had no problem completing it.

My son, on the other hand had no interest in becoming a teacher. He was more interested in playing ball with his friends. Homework was an unnecessary time waster for him. My wife and I had to make rules for him to follow that made sure that he did his homework. Often he would say that he did his homework in class. If he did not do it, he had concocted a ready story for the teacher. Being a teacher and Principal of an elementary school, I had heard all the excuses. My wife and I were very strict with him. He often complained that we were not as strict with his sister. That was true, but we didn't have to be as strict with her.

Therefore, when parents or teachers would see me to discuss the evils and or the benefits of homework, I had a personal experience that I could relate to. Little by little, I was able to get most of the teachers to agree with my "Homework by Prescription" idea. I never forced any teacher to buy into it. I felt it was far better for teachers to come to that conclusion from their own experiences.

Make homework beneficial and not just busy work.

Chapter 28

The Bi-Centennial Event

Memorize the Preamble to the Constitution

Why is it that some student groups entering Kindergarten are wonderful and others are filled with problems from day one? Those of us who have seen this phenomenon know it is true but I have never met anyone who could explain why to my satisfaction.

It so happened that one of these wonderful groups of students reached the fifth grade at the same time as the Bi-Centennial of the signing of the Constitution. From the first day of Kindergarten on, these youngsters got along with each other, helped each other, were a group you could kid with and then get right back to work with and were easy to teach. Grade after grade their teachers loved them. So, it was easy to consider taking these fifth graders on a trip to Philadelphia to celebrate the two hundredth anniversary of the signing of our country's constitution.

All four teachers of the grade loved the idea and were excited to be chaperones for this excursion. In addition, I asked three other teachers and the nurse to join us. They too were happy to be a part of what everyone agreed was to be a wonderful experience.

Plans were started early in the year in order to get the students ready for this overnight excursion. It was easy for teachers to focus their lessons on that period of time. Movies and the media were full of wonderful programs heralding the event. The students were encouraged to raise their own money for the trip by doing chores that were more than what was expected of them.

Last, but not least, I required every student to memorize the preamble to the constitution in order to qualify for a place on the bus. Each student had to come to my office and recite the entire preamble to me. They had two chances to recite it without making a mistake. Once they accomplished it, they were accepted for the trip. If they failed in the two tries, they would have to make another appointment and try again. Long before the day came, they all had succeeded in perfectly reciting the preamble to me.

Arrangements were made for the bus that would bring us there. The restaurants where we would eat, the places we would visit and the hotel where we would stay the night were also arranged. It happened that the hotel that was chosen had a swimming pool and I had mentioned it to the teachers who would be chaperoning the trip. We all thought it would be a good idea to include that in the trip information. Students and parents were told about the pool and instructed that, if interested, they would need to bring a note from home allowing them to participate in this activity. Every child brought an acceptance note!

The day came. We boarded the bus at 5:30 in the morning to get an early arrival in Philadelphia. I thought we would all catch up on our sleep during the bus ride. The kids sang the whole way down!

We visited the historic places we had all learned about, saving Constitutional Hall for last. The guide began talking about the events that took place in this magnificent building.

At one point, I asked the guide if it was okay if we as a class recited something. He said, "Sure." In unison, we recited the preamble to the Constitution. *We the People of the United States, in Order to form a more perfect Union,...* It was a great moment! The other visitors in the room clapped and cheered when we were finished. The effort we all made in preparation was well worth it. I often wonder if the students who had to memorize the preamble still remember it.

Night came and we left Philadelphia feeling very patriotic. We made our way to the Amish Country where we had a "Good and Plenty" dinner and then on to the hotel. It was 8 p.m. when we arrived at the hotel. We all had a long, active day. We were all ready for sleep. All the adults that is! The kids were ready to go. They reminded me that they had not gone swimming yet. "A promise is a promise," they said and they were right. "Okay! Change into bathing suits and meet in the corridor outside your rooms with your towels."

Once all were in the corridor, I called upon my camp counselor's experience to set the rules. "No running, no jumping into the pool, no splashing people who don't want to be splashed. You will all choose a "buddy" and when I blow the whistle you will stop what you are doing and hold up your buddy's hand. If you break any rule, you and your buddy will be out of the pool."

Having explained all the rules, we led the kids to the pool. The pool was rather large. The walls were made of tile and the sound immediately rose to a crescendo as we opened the door and walked into the pool area.

The eight teachers were stationed around the pool and I was treading water in the deep end. The kids were enjoying this wonderful experience. Not five minutes went by when a boy jumped into the deep end of the pool. I glared at him and told him to get his buddy and get out of the pool. No argument, they apologized and climbed out of the pool.

Not two minutes later, a girl jumped into the pool. "Out!" I said pointing to the two boys sitting on a bench out of the pool. The girl started to protest but there would be no discussion. "Out!" I said in a more authoritative voice and she began climbing out of the pool.

With that a boy came swimming over to me and said, "Mr. Schiffman, that girl isn't in our class!" How embarrassing was that? Thinking quickly I said, "Okay everybody can get back in the pool."

The entire trip was a huge success but…

The following year's class was so bad I wouldn't take them across the street! Go Figure!

Chapter 29

Boys Born In November

Hold Them Back?

For many years those of us who saw the differences between boys and girls entering Kindergarten would have the boys cutoff date be six months later than girls. It is clear that among five-year olds, girls were at least six months ahead of boys in language skills. Having said that the suggestion to delay the starting date for boys always fell on deaf ears.

Year after year, I visited the first grade Pacing Class to do a class observation. The problems that developed as a result of being a boy and born just before the cutoff date for entering Kindergarten was obvious. (See Chapter 5 - The Pacing Class) It reinforced my contention that the boys cut off date for Kindergarten should be six months later than girls.

The advice I formulated was reinforced from my own personal experience. Being born in March, I began Kindergarten in mid-year. At that time, schools in New York City followed the half-year system of 1A to 1B. My mother taught me how to read so I was ahead of the curriculum for 1A. The principal made the decision that I "skip" 1B and move ahead to 2A after completing 1A. That way I would be graduated in June.

The idea sounded good to my mother and she went along with it. However, that made me the youngest student in the 2A. It didn't have a negative effect on me with regard to academics but it certainly worked against me in athletics. I was up to a year younger than the boys I was competing with. It also affected my social life when I got to high school. Older girls were not looking to date younger guys!

That and many other experiences lead me to believe that the best way to deal with this problem was to "Hold Them Back". Let boys wait a year to start school. I felt so strongly about this that I would speak to all parents who were about to register their November Born Boys for Kindergarten. I would advise them to consider holding them back until the following year. Some agreed some did not but I felt I needed to explain the option to them.

A good example of this follows.

Sharon was our Art teacher for many years. During her tenure, she became pregnant and had her first child. Russ was born in November. Kidding, I chided her for the poor planning she and her husband exhibited for having a boy born in November. Years passed when Sharon questioned me about registering her son for Kindergarten. My advice remained the same. "He would be better off as a big fish in a small pond in next year's Kindergarten. Hold him back!"

She told me he attended a pre-school and was very bright. She asked if he would be bored the following year in Kindergarten. I related what my wife's and my decision was relative to our own daughter. There was a way to start our daughter in Kindergarten a year earlier than she was scheduled for.

She was born just days after the cutoff date but it could be worked out. We said, "No' and we let her begin the following year. Susan was tall for her age, very smart, and never bored. School came easy to her. Her teachers loved her and often made her the class monitor. She helped other classmates with their school problems. In the later grades, she was chosen for gifted programs. Those are not things that make for boredom.

Sharon gave it a great deal of thought. There were those who tried to convince her that Russ could handle it. They were right but he could handle it better the following year. She finally made the decision. She would hold him back!

Now I felt somewhat responsible for how he would turn out. I kept up to date on Russ' progress through his school career and afterwards. He proved me right every time. He is a very successful, married man with a child and a great job. The best stories about the advantages of being the oldest in his class happened when he got his driver's license before any of his classmates.

Holding back can have other rewards.

Chapter 30

Teachers Who Have the Magic

Nancy, A Fifth Grade Teacher

One day Nancy came to my office looking for an idea for how she could spice up her lessons. I recalled a project that I had done years ago with my fifth grade class. I brought a newspaper into the classroom and read aloud the articles that I thought would be of interest to them. The students looked forward to hearing me read to them and I enjoyed their interest.

Nancy's eyes lit up. She loved the idea. We continued to talk about the possibilities of this idea and it grew in scope until it became a major project. The plan was to put away the textbooks for three weeks and just use a newspaper to teach the curriculum. We chose Newsday, a Long Island newspaper, for what was to be used in place of the textbooks. Twenty-five Newspapers would be delivered Monday to Friday for three weeks. The more we talked about it the better we liked it. By the end of our talk, we couldn't wait to get started.

My part of the bargain was to get the newspapers delivered to the school each morning at a reduced price. Meanwhile, Nancy would work up the lessons. I called the offices at Newsday. There was excitement in my voice as I explained the project to them. I explained that an outstanding fifth grade teacher was going to undertake a project using their newspaper in place of textbooks. The answer I received almost took the wind out of my sails. "Sorry, we do that for high school students but not for fifth graders."

I was not going to disappoint Nancy or the kids or myself by giving up. I pressed on making my case and extolling the benefits that will be accrued for the newspaper as well the class. "These students are your future readers and will spread the word of how interesting your newspaper is for other kids to read." I persisted and was passed along to a number of people until I reached the top executive in the office of Public Relations. He finally agreed to give it a try!

I think the reason for his agreement was more to get me to stop the phone calls than for my rational explanations. He agreed to send us the newspapers free of charge. It was easier to do it for free rather than reduce the charges. All I would need to do was pay the driver who delivered them. Done! In return for this good deal, I promised to send him the results of the project. I couldn't wait to tell Nancy the good news.

Nancy, in the meantime, was developing lesson plans that included teaching reading, writing, spelling, arithmetic, science, geography and social studies using the articles in Newsday. It soon became apparent that the newspaper had something interesting for all these subjects. Reading, writing and spelling is obvious. For arithmetic, geography and science the class would do a weather project. It would include local weather as well as for the entire country using graphs and predictions. Social Studies was included using the current events that would also be seen on TV that night.

Twenty-five newspapers were waiting for us that Monday morning. Nancy started right in handing out the newspapers. They went over each section of the paper. That sparked the interest of the kids. They looked at the front-page headline and saw how it led readers to the article. They went on to discover the sports pages, the weather page, the comics, the TV page, the movie pages and many others. By the end of the first day, the students and Nancy were anxious to go.

Then Nancy told them that they could put their books away because they would be using the newspaper in place of their textbooks. The kids cheered!

After one week, and to the delight of their parents, the kids were able to join in on the current events discussions over dinner. That made them and their parents proud of their school lessons. Praises from the parents started coming to Nancy. They were thrilled to hear the interest in current happenings that their child displayed.

Each day brought new ideas for projects that the kids eagerly attacked. Two youngsters from Nancy's class made an appointment to interview me. I agreed and was thrilled as the two, well prepared students, conducted the interview. One asked me questions while the other took notes. I was asked questions that related to the school and the part I played as the principal. They were a little nervous at the beginning but due to their excellent preparation, they soon got into it.

Other teams interviewed every other member of the staff. They had been trained to behave in a very professional manner and ask pertinent questions. Nancy had seen to every detail. She even made up Press Cards for them to proudly display.

The three weeks flew by. As a culminating activity, they produced their own newspaper. They named it "Newsday Junior". Groups worked on their own section to put their paper together. Their paper included many of the things found in Newsday like jokes, a weather report, a crossword puzzle, that week's school lunch menu, interesting activities being done in other classes and of course, the interviews, just to name a few. It took a lot of work and the magic of Nancy to complete the tasks but it was a most wonderful experience for all concerned.

As promised, we sent a letter and a copy of "Newsday Junior" to the public relations officer at Newsday. In it, Nancy thanked him for providing the newspapers and outlined the many ways she used the newspaper to teach a variety of subjects that were part of the curriculum.

After a few days, I received a phone call from a secretary at Newsday. She said everyone there loved Newsday Junior and they wanted to set up an appointment for Nancy and me to attend a luncheon with some Newsday executives to discuss the project. Nancy and I were pleased to share the information and a meeting was arranged.

We arrived at Newsday's headquarters on the appointed day. We were escorted to the executive dining room that was filled with delectable items for lunch. Sitting around a large table were a number of well-dressed people all interested in our project. They each had a copy of the Newsday Junior we had sent. After wining and dining us, they began to ask questions about the project. "How did you come up with the idea?" "How did the students like the work?" "How did you weave the curriculum into the project?" "What was the parent reaction to the project?" The more we answered questions the more they questioned.

Finally, we all had enough. The head person assured Nancy and me that they would provide newspapers for any further projects we might have. We thanked each other and left for home. I can't explain the high that Nancy and I experienced. All the way back to school, and to this day, Nancy and I recall the events of that afternoon.

The Sequel: Newsday took the ideas gleaned from the project and started their own project. It appears in the newspaper on a regular basis. They call it "Kidsday". Nancy and I received a letter that I still have, thanking us for what we started.

Arnold, Linahan& Smith

There were three Special Education classes when I arrived at the John F. Kennedy School. Mrs. Arnold taught the youngest group, Miss Linahan the middle and Dora Smith the oldest group. Arnold, Linahan and Smith? It sounded like a law firm. They were well trained to accommodate the needs of children who scored between 50 and 75 on an IQ test. In the 1960s, they were called the E.M.R. classes. E.M.R. was an acronym for Educable Mental Retarded. There were other criteria used to make the determination for placement as well. JFK was home to the elementary aged students for the entire district. The classes could not be larger than 12 but most were less than 10. The curriculum was designed to teach the basic reading, writing and arithmetic skills they would need to know.

Dora came from Oklahoma and was in her fifties. She was a tall, thin woman who spoke with a beautiful Oklahoman accent. She took her assignment very seriously and one could see that she loved the kids and her job. The kids in turn loved her. It was a very successful, symbiotic relationship.

I was curious as to how she came to the district from Oklahoma. It seems that the retirement income in Oklahoma was fairly meager. The remuneration was not enough for her to live on. Someone told her that she could teach for 15 years in New York State and receive a pension that would make up the difference.

At the time, she was caring for her mother who was 80. She told me that she had asked her sister to care for her mother for the 15 years she would be in New York and then she would return to be the caretaker. I did the arithmetic in my head as we spoke. The plan would make her mother 95 when Dora would receive her New York State pension. I could not believe that her sister would accept this arrangement, but Dora assured me that there was a good deal of longevity in her family. Still, what were the chances of her mother living beyond 95?

I noticed that the three E.M.R. classes had little or no contact with the rest of the classes. The three classes were located at the far end of the building. They all ate lunch together with their teacher, separated from the others in the cafeteria and did not go to the playground after lunch.

I asked Dora why this was the case? She said the other kids would make fun of her kids and she didn't want to expose them to ridicule. I asked her how her kids were ever going to learn how to cope with the problems in the "Real World" "Wouldn't it be better if they learned how to deal with the possibility of ridicule here in school where you could help them?" After a while, we decided to meet with the other two teachers to discuss the issues.

After many concerns were discussed, we agreed to try something different. We would have their kids eat lunch and go to the playground with their age group. Each day their teachers would talk to them about what was happening and offer suggestions for how to deal with any problems that arose. They cautiously agreed to try it for two weeks providing that if after the trial period it was found not to be working we would return to the previous plan.

On the following Monday the youngest group ate lunch and went to the playground with the Kindergarten and first grade. The middle group went with the second and third grade and the oldest group with the fourth and fifth graders. The E.M.R. class teachers were not to be in the lunchroom or on the playground. The cafeteria aides were informed of the plan and kept a special eye on the E.M.R. kids.

I am not going to tell you that there were no problems, but their teachers were able to show them how to deal with them. After the two-week trial period, it was clear that the plan was working. The taunting, if any, that occurred on the first few days had stopped. By the end of the second week the E.M.R. kids were eating and playing with their new friends. The kids were great!

I had formed a special relationship and respect for Dora. She was an elegant lady. When she walked through the halls with her kids they followed her like baby ducklings following their mother. Her kids were always well behaved. One day I jokingly asked her where she kept the gun that kept the kids so well behaved. Her serious answer was, "I love these children and they know it. They wouldn't do anything that would disappoint me. I tell them how I expect them to behave before we go anyplace and they do." I never forgot that.

For the record, her mother lived to 103.

Sequel: Dora finished her fifteen years and returned to her small town in Oklahoma. One day the news media told of a major tornado that had gone through the town that Dora lived in. I was quite concerned and wanted to find out if she was okay. The problem was that we didn't have her phone number. What were the chances of a telephone operator finding a Smith's phone number? I decided to try "Information" anyway. I dialed 411 and requested the town and state where she lived. An operator answered with the same Oklahoma accent as Dora's. I asked for the phone number of a "Dora Smith" explaining that I did not know her address. She must have sensed the concern in my voice. To my amazement the operator said, "Dora? She's okay! The tornado missed her house." Talk about a small town in a small world! She connected me with Dora and we spoke for a while. Her mother was still alive and they both were doing well.

Poetry By Nancy Woronowich. Art For Your Ears

I asked Nancy if she would like to contribute to this effort by writing about her poetry unit? This is the way a Master Teacher thinks:

"Sometimes terrific ideas for units just seem to come to me while riding home from work, watching TV or relaxing with a good book. Other ideas just begin as part of the basic curriculum. As I continue to teach the unit it evolves into something my students and I feel is worth perusing. That was the way my unit on poetry developed.

My first recollection of poetry beyond nursery rhymes was when I was a student in a middle school. We had a large textbook called 'Prose and Poetry'. I really don't remember a single poem from that book. My thoughts as I look back are, "Couldn't the teacher find at least one memorable poem for us to read?" I might as well have been in a class that was taught in a foreign language for all that I got out of that poetry class. Well, I actually did come away from that class with one new idea and that was "I HATE POETRY!"

I was never made to feel that any thoughts I had about the meaning of a poem were acceptable. The teacher would have us read the poem and then we were asked what we thought? If we weren't thinking the 'right' thoughts, we needed to correct our 'thinking' or flunk the next exam. Another 'fun' part of poetry way back then was memorizing the prologue to the Canterbury Tales, in Old English no less. The teacher set a time limit for how long we had to memorize it.

One day in 2003, I came across a poem written by the Poet Laureate, Billy Collins. His poem expressed exactly how teachers had ruined poetry for me.

Introduction to Poetry by Billy Collins:

I ask them to take a poem

and hold it up to the light

like a color slide or press an ear against its hive

I say drop a mouse into a poem and watch him probe his way out,

or walk inside the poem's room and feel the walls for a light switch.

I want them to water-ski across the surface of a poem

waving at the author's name on the other shore.

But all they want to do is tie the poem to a chair with rope

and torture a confession out of it. They begin beating it with a hose

to find out what it really means.

*When I started to teach poetry to my students, it was merely part of the curriculum and I did not have any excitement in my heart for it. I would teach the unit and move on. But I wanted so much to make learning poetry fun and enjoyable and not to **"torture a confession out of it"**. Each year I added something a little special to my unit and dropped something that was boring out of it. I started to accumulate poems that the children really enjoyed. I would read the selected poems aloud to the class.*

My biggest challenge was to find a way to give the children a good understanding and true appreciation for what poetry was all about. I took classes and asked the questions that were meant to fix things that bothered me about poetry. Not that I ever got two of the same answers but it made me understand that poetry is what I now call "Art For Your Ears". Some things just are the way the poet wants them to be.

Once I began to feel comfortable with poetry myself, I was able to share that with the children. I have taught Haikus because they are short and beautiful and don't have to rhyme; acrostics, because once the children get the hang of it they can have a lot of fun creating them; couplets, triplets and quatrains to show children different rhyming patterns. I have had children write their autobiographies using quatrains. We learned cinquains, diamantes, even sonnets.

I also wanted the children to hear the writings of some of the better-known poets. So the children each brought a notebook to class and everyday I would read a few poems by well-known authors. Every page in their notebook had the name of one of these poets at the top of the page. When I would read a poem by a particular author the children would write the title on the author's page. When I finished reading, we would discuss the poem and the children would give it a 1-10 rating. Over time the children started to realize that they had 'favorite' poets – who would have thought??? Of course Shel Silverstein was an expected favorite but one day a child told me that he really liked Langston Hughes. Now I was really impressed.

So many other activities can be used to validate each child's poem. I would frequently enter children's poems into contests. We wrote a class anthology that won first place at the Walt Whitman Poetry Contest. We made a class book of poems with children submitting their best works. For National Poetry Month students read their poems aloud in the cafeteria during their lunch hour.

In teaching poetry, I learned that children have very fragile egos. I realized that if I wasn't sincere and kind to the students as I tried to direct their learning in an abstract subject like poetry, they could easily lose interest for a very long time. I never graded children on the poems they wrote. They learned and improved through my lessons, my gentle feedback and the feedback of others. I hope my students gained an appreciation for poetry that still lives with them today."

Thank you Nancy!

Chapter 31

Important Decisions

The Team Approach

One of the most important lessons I learned from my mentor was "Don't take someone else's problems!" From time to time, a fellow principal tried to unload a problem teacher onto me. Whenever I received a call like that, I thought of those words and said "No thanks." But when the Superintendent asks you to take on a problem teacher, you have little choice.

That's exactly what happened. I got a call from the superintendent asking me to take a different speech specialist. I knew whom he meant. Everyone knew the one I was getting could be a major problem. I tried to beg off but he said that I was the only one who could "control" her misbehavior. I finally had to accept.

To her credit, Mrs. J is a very intelligent, well-educated person. When she did her job, she did it well. The problem was that she didn't always do her job. Other specialists would come to the classroom, collect the youngsters and escort them to their room. Not Mrs. J! Teachers told me they would get their kids ready and Mrs. J would not come to get them. The kids would miss all or part of their lesson.

I asked Mrs. J about this and she told me she decided that the children who came to her for training should know when to come on their own. She claimed it was part of her lesson. Some of these children were only six or seven year-olds.

I told her it had nothing to do with her training and that she should please check with me before initiating any new rules. She totally agreed! I was satisfied.

A week later, I heard from a first grade teacher that Mrs. J was still not coming to pick up her students. She would call but when told that she was supposed to walk the child to her room she refused and the children missed the lesson.

Once again, I spoke to Mrs. J and told her that the school rule was for all special teachers to accompany the younger children to her room and back when the lesson was done. This was a safety procedure. She totally agreed! No argument! Somehow, I didn't feel as satisfied this time.

Time after time a teacher would tell me of something that Mrs. J did or didn't do that was not according to protocol. Time after time, I would speak to her about what was expected. Time after time, she would totally agree! She never argued!

One day a classroom teacher came to me to relate a conversation she had with the parent of one of her students. The parent thought her child had a speech problem and needed the services of the speech teacher. The classroom teacher did not feel the child had a serious problem, and that pulling her out of class to attend a lesson would do the child more harm than good. Just to cover all the bases we decided to put through a request for a speech evaluation. The necessary forms were sent out and, within a week, the evaluation was completed.

Soon after the evaluation, I met with the classroom teacher, the speech teacher and some other teachers who knew the student. We discussed the issues. The speech teacher's evaluation was that the student had a slight problem but it was the kind that would be outgrown. Her recommendation was to wait and see. Everyone agreed to wait and see and we would explain our reasoning to the parent.

The classroom teacher, the speech teacher and I met with the parents. I explained that our program was designed for children whose problems were much more serious than what her daughter exhibited. I also told the parents that what we had was a pullout program so their daughter would miss some class time during the time she attended the speech class. I assured them that the speech teacher would check on her progress from time to time to see if conditions changed. The parents agreed, thanked everyone and stood to leave.

The meeting was about to end when Mrs. J interjected, "I think a six month remedial program is warranted at this time." I couldn't believe what I just heard! I tried to keep a poker face as the parents turned around, looking a bit confused. Now the meeting went from them leaving to them listening to the speech teacher, who had been silent during the meeting. She went on to explain the program she would do with the child and how her plan would be sure to help.

The parents glared at me! Who was I to deny service when the expert's recommendation was different from mine? I was speechless! In the next few minutes, we scheduled a time for the girl to receive remediation for her problem. I was tempted to tell the parents not to worry about missing class-time, because she would probably not get to attend the sessions very often anyway. But I held my tongue.

The parents and classroom teacher left. I asked Mrs. J to remain. When we were alone and I was sure the parents could not hear me I closed the door and shouted, "What the (blank) was that about? I thought we agreed on what to do!"

She kept her cool and said, "Yes, but I changed my mind." Many thoughts crossed my mind. Some I cannot put into print. I realized that whatever I said at that moment would be wrong so I just pointed to the door and told her to get out! "I am too angry to deal with this now." Mrs. J left, I stewed! I decided to write up the incident and deal with it when I was much cooler.

The following day I received a package from Mrs. J. For a moment, I listened to hear if the package was ticking. When I opened it there was a book titled "I'm Ok—You're Ok" By Harris Thomas Anthony. That summed it all up. There was no way I was ever going to "control" her. She would never argue or even disagree. She would agree and then do whatever she pleased. When my psychologist friend heard some of the stories he laughingly said, "You are dealing with a passive/aggressive personality. They are very hard to deal with." The strange thing is that with all the problems I had with her, I liked her! She was basically a good person.

The next day I called the Superintendent and told him that he had too much faith in me. After telling him some of the stories, I told him I had to surrender. Mrs. J beat me as she had all the others. He told me she had been moved around quite a bit and nobody wanted her so, "Do the best you can."

I decided to get on her case. I looked at a copy of her schedule and made sure she stuck to it. On one of the days, she came to our school in the afternoon after servicing the school next door. She took one hour and thirty minutes for lunch and driving to our school. The school she came from shared the same parcel of land as ours. It just meant she had to make a right turn at the corner and park her car in our lot.

I called her into my office and told her she was entitled to a forty-five minute lunch time and no more than fifteen minutes to get to her next scheduled class. "That equals one hour!" "But" she said, "what if the traffic light at the corner is red when I get to it?" I was not prepared for that answer but suddenly I remembered that the "right turn on red" law had recently been enacted. Would you believe I told her that now she wouldn't have to wait for the light to change. She could make a right turn even if the light was red. I don't know who was nuttier!

There were many incidents where I made sure she did what she was paid to do. Any time she didn't, I wrote the incident up and, after showing it to her, I put it in her personnel folder. After a while, I noticed that she was starting to feel the pressure. I decided to sit with her and just have a talk. "You don't like being watched and made to toe the line any more than I like being on your case." I said. She agreed. I asked her if she was considering retirement. She was beyond the minimum age and was eligible to collect her pension. She thought for a minute and said, "I will think about it." I decided to sweeten the pot. "If you decide to retire at the end of this year and you put your retirement papers in, I will get off your case for the remainder of the year. What's more I will see to it that everyone else gets off your case as well." She seemed to like the idea. "But" I said, "You have to show me a plan that you have for when you retire so that you won't change your mind at the last minute."

A few weeks later, she told me she would put her retirement papers in and she had a plan. It seems that a relative of hers owned a movie theater and he was ready to sell it to her. "That is some plan!" I thought. "It's a deal," I said. "No one will give you a hard time for the rest of the school year."

Whenever anyone came to me with a complaint about her I would simply say, "Just be patient! It will all be better soon." I stuck to my part of the bargain and she stuck to hers. The end of the year came and we said, "Goodbye."

Sequel: To the best of my knowledge the Teacher turned movie-theater owner did very well. She and her husband showed movies that were more avant-garde than those shown in the regular theaters.

One day an article appeared in the local newspaper and there she was. The article was about Mrs. J and the theater. It seems that she had a rule against patrons bringing food or drink into the theater. They had a food court where people could purchase candy or other items.

The article related a story about a man who came to the theater with some sort of hard candy to suck on. The owner of the theater told the man that he was not permitted to bring that item into the theater and he would have to give it up. The man objected. One thing led to another and the police were summoned. The man was ejected and the story made the newspaper.

Roll ahead many years. I was on line at a movie theater in Boca Raton, Florida waiting to purchase tickets for the movie. Two couples in front of me were talking loud enough for me to overhear their conversation. The man was relating an incident that happened long ago on Long Island where he was ejected from a movie theater for bringing cough drops into the theater that were not allowed by the owner. He confessed that he did not remember her name.

Without any introduction, I simply said the theater owner's name. The four people turned to see who had spoken that name. The man said, "That's the name! I was the guy she threw out of the theater that day. How did you know her?" I went on to tell him the story and we all had a good laugh.

The Team Approach is best, providing every member is on the team!

Chapter 32

Teachers Who Are Hard On Kids

A Reputation Once Established Is Hard To Change

I am sure that due to my own experience with a teacher who was "hard on me", I was particularly concerned with any teacher who had that reputation. "She is mean" is the most common expression used by kids who are afraid of their teacher. When I started teaching and even when I became a principal the paddle was used by principals to hit misbehaving children. Bad enough when it was used for disciplinary reasons but it was even used as punishment for turning in poor work. Learning should be taught with excitement and fun not fear.

Most often, an overly strict teacher does it for control. They fear that they would lose control of the class if they smiled, let alone joked, with the kids. As a student teacher I was told by one of these teachers "Don't even smile until Thanksgiving!" I am happy to say that I didn't listen to his advice. There are better ways to keep control without using intimidation or being "mean".

No sooner had I become Principal than I was made aware of a teacher who was known by the kids as being "mean". I decided to observe her lesson as soon as possible. At our pre-observation conference, she was precise and well prepared. She explained what the lesson was about and how she would be going about presenting it. Her exactness only increased my concern that she was using methods of intimidation in her teaching.

The day came and I readied myself to find support for my preconceived idea of what I would see and hear. I expected to find a poor teacher who had to use fear to maintain discipline. Instead, I found a very good teacher who was overly strict but fair. Her lesson was as well prepared as our pre-conference. More importantly, the kids were paying attention. When students didn't understand something, they would raise their hand and wait to be called upon. Then they would ask their question. The answer they got was clear and had no hint of ridicule. When she was satisfied that her answer was understood she went on with the lesson. The lesson included all the elements of what a good lesson should contain.

The more I watched her teach the more I realized that with a little direction she could be a master teacher. I did a 180-degree turn around in my thinking. I couldn't wait to tell her how impressed I was with her lesson. But, I still had to talk to her about her reputation for being considered "Mean".

At our post-conference, she admitted knowing that she had the reputation of being "Mean". She too had been told that she had to be tough with the kids for the first few months of the year. No smiles, no jokes, just serious business. That was her experience when she attended school and that's how she was going to run her class! We talked about the difference between being "strict" and being "mean". She was certainly not mean! "So" I said, "Let's get rid of the 'Mean' reputation and modify the 'Strict' methods you use to keep control. Your lessons are so well prepared and delivered that you don't have to be so strict to maintain control."

Within months, her methods changed and she became more moderate. She even smiled and joked with the kids.

Her thought of as being "mean" reputation however, remained for many years. When parents saw her room number on their child's report card, some would come to me asking that their child be transferred to a different teacher. I had to convince parents that she had changed and to give her a chance to prove it. I would say that if they felt the same way after two weeks I would make the change.

I'm happy to say that I never received a request for change. In fact, many made it their business to tell me how happy their child was.

Some things can be fixed

Some Cannot

I know I am repeating myself but it needs to be repeated. A principal's first concern is for the welfare of all the students!

This story took place in the late 1960s. Times were very different then than they are today. Behavior that was considered strange or quirky but accepted then would not be tolerated today. Teachers and administrators are much more cautious when it comes to being affectionate with children. Of all the problems that I faced as a principal, this has had the most lasting impact on my memory.

The teacher in this story came to me with a reputation of being very friendly with students. The students seemed happy with the teaching methods he used and learning was taking place.

From time to time, I would notice behavior that crossed the line from friendly to too familiar. We spoke about these behaviors and the teacher always assured me that it was, "just done in fun". Without going into detail, I began to suspect that this "very friendly teacher" was crossing the line often. Some of these behaviors could even be considered to be of a sexual nature. When I described these behaviors to a psychologist friend of mine he said I was right in being concerned. "These are very suspect behaviors that could indicate a serious problem."

An incident involving an after school intramural event run by this teacher was brought to my attention by the boy's father. The boy was required to strip down to his underwear in order to get to his locker after being last in a race in the gym.

I made an appointment with the assistant superintendent and related the many suspected behaviors that concerned me. He agreed that these allegations could be very serious and we set about to plan for how to proceed. I would keep a written record of every suspected behavior and bring each to the attention of the teacher. It would include what I said and his response. The written description of the event would be placed in his permanent folder. It became evident that this teacher's behavior had often crossed the line.

The Assistant Superintendent and I brought the matter to the attention of the Superintendent and the Board of Education. It was clear that this would be a legal matter and we should be sure to adhere to the law. The school attorneys were consulted and it was decided that the parents of the children who had been involved in a questionable issue should be advised and asked if they would testify in court if it came to that.

The school attorney and I interviewed the parents of students who had a questionable experience with this teacher. They all were angry and wanted something done, but not one of them wanted their child to testify in court. No matter how the attorney tried, he could not get a single parent to agree to have their child testify if necessary. Be advised, it is much easier to recognize deviant behavior than it is to be able to prove it in a court of law. The school attorneys advised against bringing the case to court.

My concern was first to protect the kids and that we should pursue the case even if we lost it. I was told instead to, "Keep an eye on the teacher's behavior." I strenuously objected to this plan saying that I could not do my job with the rest of the school if I were responsible for watching him.

The ultimate decision of the board and the Superintendent was to transfer him to the Junior High School. I was not in favor of that decision and wrote a letter detailing all the suspected behaviors that I had recorded. I sent that letter to the Board and the Superintendent and added that, "In the event a parent sued the district on behalf of a child that was harmed, I would testify on behalf of the student." That letter did not make me any friends at Central, but it had to be said.

Twenty years passed. The new Superintendent summoned me to his office. He showed me the letter I had written twenty years ago. He asked if I remembered writing the letter. I looked at it and all the memories of that event came flooding back. I told him that I remembered every word.

He related a story that was told to him by a parent who came to his office inquiring about this same teacher. When he was told that this teacher was still working in the district, the parent told him that he had been "sodomized" by this teacher. He went on to say, "Those memories haunt me to this day and I don't want any other kid to suffer as I have."

This time the issue was brought to the attention of the police. A wire was used to get an admission of guilt from the teacher. There was no doubt as to what had happened and the teacher was severely punished.

I should feel vindicated by the end of this story but it also saddens me. I still wonder how many kids have grown up with memories that haunt them as a result of this teacher. It took too long to get resolved. Today at the first sign of suspicious behavior, it must be brought to the attention of the principal. The principal is then required by law to report the incident to the authorities and Protective Services.

Where do you draw the line between "friendly" and "overly friendly" with students? Sometimes it is difficult to tell. As a result,

A pat on the back that is called for may not be delivered.

Chapter 33

Interviewing and Hiring

One of the most important tasks an administrator must do is to hire a great staff. A good teacher will cause a principal few if any problems. A poor one causes continual headaches. The same goes for hiring principals and central administrators.

Hiring A Principal:

Attention to detail, from the resume to the hiring:

As the Assistant Superintendent, one of my responsibilities was to find and recommend the hiring of personnel. My first hiring assignment came when the then junior high school principal announced his retirement. A new person was needed to lead the school.

The interview and selection process that eventually got to the actual hiring taught me a lot about how to go about being interviewed. The first thing I realized was that going through scores of resumes in an effort to finally select a few to be interviewed was a tremendous chore. No matter what system was used, the odds were slim that a resume would make it to the final cut.

The procedure:

An advertisement was placed in the New York Times and local newspapers and the applications rolled in. They kept coming until the deadline, after which we stopped collecting them. At final count, they numbered 168. I shuddered looking at the boxes filled with people's hopes and dreams that were stacked up in the corner of my office. How was I going to read through all these resumes and select the one best person for the job?

The plan:

I met with the junior high school teachers. We talked about the qualities that the next principal would need in order to bring the school to the standard they all sought. Using the suggestions made by the junior high school teachers, eight people were selected as the committee to review the resumes. The committee was made up of six junior high teachers, the senior high principal and me.

The process:

At our first meeting, we created a template for how to evaluate each resume. We listed all the items that we felt would be important for our future principal to possess. We looked at experience, education, quality of writing and the appearance of their application just to name a few. Some items were more important than others so we gave them a greater weighting. Each member was given 20 resumes to score. We used the eight remaining resumes to refine the scoring template.

For practice, and in order to get some consistency, we each scored one of the eight resumes arriving at a final number. Discussion and compromise continued to refine the template. We then re-scored the eight resumes. Just to be certain that one person did not miss something, each of the eight resumes was read and scored by two people. Any time there was a significant difference between the two scores, that resume was pulled and read by a third person. When all of us scored the resumes with a similar score, we got to work.

The first cut:

The first cut was quick and easy. Those who did not have the qualifications, and those resumes that were not written perfectly went into the "out" file. Things like misspellings or punctuation errors went quickly to that "out" file. That still left too many. The committee decided that experience was important so we eliminated those who had no administrative experience. Next, their experience had to be close to that which is best suited to a junior high school principal. We still had a large number but it was starting to look manageable.

The cut to 20:

When we got down to the last 20 we realized that any one of them could possibly be the best for the job but how to tell who was best? Since it is not reasonable to interview 20, we started looking for the "Grabber". The grabber is that line or two in the resume that stands out and would get the reader's attention. An interesting job: "I worked with a circus for one summer." That's a grabber! "I taught 12 year olds in Kenya for a year." "I climbed Mount Everest." These have nothing to do with the qualifications needed for a junior high school principal but they pique interest and cause the reader to pause and look further. That's what you want your resume to do! If you don't have a grabber, Go, Get One! Yes, go out and do something out of the ordinary. Volunteer, learn something special, write articles and try to get them published. Whatever it is, try to make it a grabber. Hopefully your resume will do what it is intended to do and that is to get you an interview.

Getting ready for the interview:

At the next meeting, we chose the people with the top ten scores and put them into the interview file. The people who submitted the other 158 resumes were sent a letter thanking them for applying. I always felt those that took the time to apply deserved an answer. The top ten applicants were then invited to the first, formal interview.

The First Formal Interview:

Our next task was to establish the interview process. Once again, we listed the attributes and created a profile for the "perfect" candidate. We brainstormed for how to find ways to get the best picture of each candidate and how that candidate matched up with our standards.

The plan was for six of us to interview each candidate at the same time. The other two remained at the junior high and would act as host for any who chose to visit the school. Each candidate was given the opportunity to visit the school before coming to the interview. A host would escort the candidate around the building and answer any questions they may have. Take advantage of this opportunity. Candidates who did were very appealing to the committee. The opinions expressed by their hosts carried a lot of weight.

The rest of us had pre-set questions that we asked each candidate. Additional questions could be asked by the interviewers to gain more information. We were looking for the candidate's demeanor as well as the quality of the answers given so as to see how they fit the profile.

We wanted the candidate to feel relaxed so we included questions that stimulated dialogue such as:

*Who in your life influenced you in choosing education as your profession, and describe the part they played?

*Looking back at your educational accomplishments, what project or decision that you were responsible for are you most proud of and why?

*Describe the school in which you are currently working and your role there.

*What, if any, are problems at your school and how are you involved in handling them?

Above all, there were no questions meant to produce pressure. If you have ever been interviewed for a position that you wanted you know how much pressure you were already experiencing. Besides, we felt it was more important to see how people responded when they were relaxed rather than when they were uptight.

The interviews were scheduled and conducted. At the end of the day, all eight of us met. The six interviewers and two hosts shared their impressions of each candidate. That narrowed the number to five.

The final cut:

Till now the process could be considered fairly routine. The last part of the plan proved to be very deciding. We informed the five finalists of their status and requested that the Superintendent and I be invited to visit their school. At each of the schools, we looked to see that what the candidate had said at the interview was what was happening at their school. That eliminated one candidate immediately who was a front-runner after the first interview. What he said was not what was happening. Had we not visited his school, armed with specific things to look for, he may very well have become the person chosen.

Recommendation to the Board:

The remaining four candidates were recommended for interview by the Board of Education along with the committee's top recommendation. Having heard how the committee arrived at the finalists, the Board of Education decided to go with the committee's top recommendation. They commended the committee for the work we did.

The result:

Mel Noble, the junior high assistant Principal from Carmel, NY, was chosen. Within a few weeks everyone recognized the positive changes that were initiated by him. Soon everyone agreed the school was running smoothly as a result of his leadership. He remained the principal of the Junior High for a number of years until he was promoted to Assistant Superintendent and later to Superintendent of the district.

Hard work and careful planning paid off!

Chapter 34

Time Management

The Jumping Monkey

Not every problem is yours! Some are and some are not. Know the difference and act accordingly.

Early in my career as Principal, someone asked me to explain just what a principal does. I thought about that and realized that I went from one interruption to the next. The plans I made for the day were seldom completed due to the many unplanned disruptions that occurred during the day.

People frequently came to me with their problems. I could not say "No." It may have been good for my ego and feelings of importance but not very good for the efficiency of running the school. I decided to attend a Time Management conference. At the conference, we discussed many different aspects of the problem and they all seemed to be mine. The one that made the biggest impression on me was the following:

The instructor said, "The next time a person comes to you and says, 'we have a problem' visualize a monkey sitting on that person's shoulder ready to jump to your shoulder. Once on your shoulder the problem becomes yours and there go minutes, hours or even days of your time. So as soon as you hear that 'we have a problem' phrase look to see that crouching monkey and think, does this problem belong to me or to the person who is asking for help"?

Make some suggestions if you have any. Let the person make suggestions. Offer support. Listen and commiserate. Tell them they could come back in a few days to talk about their progress. Anything, but don't let that monkey land on your shoulder."

I have given that advice to numerous people, not just teachers but others who have been bogged down at one time or another by that pesky monkey. The time spent on another person's problem is often valuable time taken away from your own personal problems. In an effort to be helpful, they allowed the monkey to become ensconced on their shoulder and then they wonder where the time went?

It is by far the advice that people most remember and tell me about when I see them years later. They tell me stories about how they thwarted a monkey that was about to leap onto their shoulder. I nod in agreement and often hear a sincere thank you that accompanies it.

To this day, I smile when I hear that 'we have a problem' phrase. I can still see that crouching monkey. That visualization has saved me countless hours of time that were better spent.

Watch out for that jumping monkey!

Chapter 35

Responsibility and Decisions

No Win Decisions.

When to close schools?

There are some decisions that are both right and wrong. When faced with those the best you can do is to make a decision and let the chips fall. One of those was when to close school due to inclement weather. Winter on Long Island means snow. When the snow starts early and is heavy, the solution is easy. Close the schools. It is when the weather report creates uncertainty that the decision gets tough.

It was 4:30 AM when the phone rang. I was awake because I had been listening to weather reports all night. The report was from 4 to 8 inches of snow. 4 inches we could handle, 8 inches we close. I dreaded that call all evening. The call was from John at the bus garage. The Superintendent was out of town at a conference and I, the Assistant Superintendent, had to make the decision for the district.

I asked John what he thought hoping he would make the decision. John simply said, "It doesn't look good but it's your call." This was exactly the answer I did not want to hear but he was exactly right. I knew that we had extra days in the calendar for just this kind of event. I also knew that there were many working people who depended on the school being open so they could go to work knowing their children were well taken care of. On the other hand, what if a child was hurt in an accident caused by the storm? If I said, "We are open" and some children were struck by a skidding car while waiting for their bus I could see the headlines, "Assistant Defies Weather Report".

I decided to err on the side of caution. "Let's close the schools John." "Okay," said John and we both began the process of informing the necessary people. I called the local radio and TV stations. Then I started the telephone chain to the teachers. All the while, I looked outside and hoped now that the snowfall would increase. Please make this a storm that made me look like I made the right decision!

By 5:30 AM all the calls were done. All the district's schools were closed! I continued to listen to the local stations and heard that some other School Districts had closed. That was a relief!

Then it happened. Without any warning, the snow stopped falling and the sun came out. The media switched from "snow storm" to "We sure dodged a bullet this time!" By 8 a.m., even the snow that had fallen was fast disappearing. "Who made this dumb decision?" That was all I could hear in my head. I drove to my office and let myself into the building. The phones were ringing. I answered and accepted the anger and chastisement for closing school when there was no need to. I didn't explain that I had made the decision at 4:30 a.m., when the snowfall was heavy and the media was calling for a storm. No one wanted to hear that. I simply apologized and hoped it did not cause too much of a problem for them. I thought about my decision and decided that with the same information I would do the same thing.

Better safe than sorry

Let The Person Responsible Make the Decision.

A parent I'll call Mrs. X came to my office one day. Her child was receiving special speech help with three other needy students three times per week. She said that her child was very shy and could not improve while sharing time with other children. She wanted her child to receive speech individually, five times per week. The rule was that only children whose speech was seriously unintelligible could receive that very expensive one-to-one help. I told Mrs. X that I would speak to the speech teacher and the classroom teacher with regard to her request and I would get back to her.

That day I spoke to both teachers and personally spoke to the child. No one thought that her speech problems warranted a one-to-one type of remediation. I called Mrs. X and explained that neither the classroom teacher nor the Speech Teacher felt her daughter needed individual speech help. The plan was to continue with the three times per week program and the speech teacher would make sure her child was involved.

Mrs. X did not accept our decision and took her case to the newly appointed Assistant Superintendent who I will call Miss Y. Miss Y listened to what Mrs. X had to say and agreed with her. Without consulting with any of us, she granted the child individual speech help five times per week. With all due respect to the new Assistant Superintendent, she didn't realize the ramifications of that decision. But she had to be made aware that making a decision without asking us at school for our input was a bad idea.

Mrs. X returned to my office with a smile on her face and the order from "my boss". I told her I would make the necessary arrangements and the new speech schedule would begin as soon as possible. If someone took my blood pressure at that moment, I would have been rushed to the hospital. This was an unfortunate example of authority without responsibility. That is the worst exercise of administrative power!

The question now was how I was going to deal with it. I decided to compose a letter addressed to the parents of all the children who were in the speech program. The letter would state that anyone who so wished could get individual speech help, five times a week for their child. They would simply have go to the new Assistant Superintendent in charge of special help and request it. I added her name, school address and phone number to the letter. I sent a CC of the letter to the Assistant Superintendent and waited.

I don't think it took 5 minutes after she received the letter for her to call me. "Jerry, what have you done?" I played it sweet and dumb. "I figured you wanted all the children to have the same opportunity to have one-to-one speech help. You don't want to give it to one child without asking the other parents if they wanted it for their child. I wrote this letter to the parents so their children could receive the same treatment as the one you agreed to with Mrs. X. As soon as you know how many parents request the change please let me know so I can arrange the new schedules and you can hire the necessary new speech teachers that will be needed."

Though I could not see her reaction to what I just said, I could certainly sense it by what she said. She blustered that was not what she meant to happen and she did not think I would inform other parents and how was she going to hire that many speech teachers and what can we (see The Monkey) do now?

I let her sweat for a while and finally told her that I had no intention of sending any letter to the parents at this time. This was just to show her what could happen. "But in the future please check with the people who have the knowledge and responsibility before exercising your authority." I think she learned a good lesson. Some time later she thanked me for teaching her how to say, "I'll check with the Principal and get back to you" just as I say,

"I'll check with the teacher and get back to you."

Policy Decisions Can Also Imprison

First, let me say that I take retention very seriously! It is a traumatic decision for the child and the family. When a teacher comes to me with a recommendation for retaining a student, he or she must prove to me that the student will definitely and significantly benefit from it. It is <u>never</u> <u>for</u> <u>punishment</u>!

First and most important! The possibility of retention should not come as a surprise to the parents at the end of the term. Parents should have been involved in the learning process throughout the year and be told what they can do to improve their child's progress.

During my meeting with the teacher, I take the roll of the parent and ask the questions that the teacher must answer. I ask the teacher to tell me that the youngster will be at least in the top half of the same grade the following year. We don't only focus on academic problems. The emotional trauma it causes for the family as well as the child is as important as the academics it proposes to benefit. Forcing retention on a student against the will of parents is doomed to failure. The benefits must outweigh the losses before we even bring the suggestion to the parents.

After the teacher makes a strong enough case to me in support of retaining a student, we can schedule a meeting with the parents. The teacher and I tell the parents that the meeting will be about placement for the following year so that they can prepare for the meeting.

At the meeting, the teacher will explain the reasons for the plan to retain their youngster. I tell the parents that in the questioning I will take the side for not retaining because I know what tough questions to ask. The teacher will have to convince both of us that retention is in the best interest of the child.

The meeting will address what the advantages and disadvantages might be. It is often a difficult meeting and should be. If, after all options are explored and there is no way the parents will buy into it, I back off. I tell them to think about the benefits and the disadvantages of promotion as well as retention and then suggest we meet again in a week. I found that if the parents are vehemently opposed to keeping their child back, the retention does not work! All you do is make an enemy. We would have to find other means for dealing with the student's academic problems. In any case, I ask all concerned to agree or disagree in writing with the decision. That way we all have a stake in it.

Having said all that, there are times when retention is advised and mutually agreed to. Our cutoff-date for beginning Kindergarten was December 1st. That meant that all five-year old children born on or before that date could legally start Kindergarten that September.

A parent came to school to register her daughter for Kindergarten. Her birthday was late in November. She explained that her daughter was born two months prematurely. Had she been a full term birth, she would have been born in January and would not be eligible for Kindergarten until the following year. But the law doesn't speak to these exceptions. She was legally eligible but not emotionally ready to attend Kindergarten that year.

Her parents knew that she was not ready to begin Kindergarten. They were looking for a way to deal with the problems. The law in New York State does not require Kindergarten registration at the age of five. I suggested placing their daughter in a pre-school program for this year and let her start Kindergarten next year. The parents said they would love to but they could not afford the expense of a pre-school. We also decided that remaining home for the year would not be in the best interest of the child.

Finally, we agreed to a plan that would have the child attend Kindergarten this year, with the understanding that she would repeat Kindergarten the following year. During the current year she would be exposed to some of the Kindergarten program but not be under any pressure to succeed. She and the family could be told that she was too young to go on to first grade. That would give plenty of time for the plan to work. She had a year to mature and be ready for Kindergarten the next year. So far so good!

In the middle of the year, at the beckoning of the Superintendent, the Board of Education instituted a "No Retention Policy" for the following year. I agreed with the concept but not the policy. There had to be room for unique circumstances to be considered. I told the Superintendent about the case of the child we were planning to retain who was now attending Kindergarten. She said I had to adhere to the policy. No matter how much I explained about the premature birth and the parent's agreement to the solution of the problem, the answer was the same. "No retentions"!

I met with the parents to discuss the new "no retention" policy decision that had been adopted. They were shocked and upset. There was no way their child was going to be ready for first grade. The Kindergarten teacher and I agreed, but I was told there would be no exceptions.

I suggested that the parent send a letter to the Superintendent explaining their unusual situation and that she and her husband planned to bring this matter to the attention of the Board of Education at the next meeting. They would explain the circumstances that lead to the decision to start their daughter in Kindergarten for that year with the understanding that she would be retained in Kindergarten the following year. They would ask the

Board to make an exception in this case to their recent "No Retention Policy".

The Superintendent apparently did not want this to go before the Board. The call came the next day. She told me to go ahead with the planned retention but for this case only. I agreed and informed the parents.

Dealing with children is different from any other situation where a product is involved. Unlike turning out widgets where one is exactly like the next, every child is different. There are no two alike! Educators can make general practices when it comes to dealing with educating children but hard and fast rules are often doomed to fail.

Policies Help In Decision Making But Exceptions Must Be Allowed For

Chapter 36

Good Results

Full-Day Kindergarten

I had just become the Principal. At the time, our Kindergarten classes were only half a day. There was a morning session and an afternoon session. On the first rainy day, I watched in horror when the morning kindergartners came to school. I knew why Kindergarten teachers prayed that it did not rain on the first day of school. There must have been a sale on yellow slickers and yellow boots at the local department store because almost every kid was wearing them.

I watched the Kindergarten teachers carefully check each child's slicker and boots to make sure the child's name was clearly marked before helping remove them to be stored in the coat closet. Teachers hurriedly printed the child's name on boots and slickers for those that contained no name while at the same time kept the others busy. After observing this the first time, I scheduled help for the Kindergarten teachers for any rainy first days of school.

Making sure the names were in and correct took a great deal of time but it was well worth the effort, for when it was time to go home they had to reverse the process. Teachers had to be sure the right slickers and boots went home on the right child. Much of the two and a half hour session was spent with the slickers and boots. It was clear that on rainy or snowy days there would be little time for teaching the curriculum.

Five year-olds are very literal! This story proves the point.

After seeing to it that each child had a slicker and boots on, the Kindergarten teacher asked if everyone had their correct outerwear. One girl raised her hand and said she did not. In a panic, the teacher checked every slicker and boot but could not find an error. At last she asked the little girl if she was sure that what she had on was not hers? The little girl, who was almost in tears said, "They're not mine, they're my brother's."

Eighteen years later I became the district's Assistant Superintendent. Our district still had half-day Kindergarten. That year New York State offered a monetary incentive for districts to change to a full-day Kindergarten program. I thought about that first day and the time it took to get the kids ready for starting and ending the day. I decided to look into the advantages and disadvantages of a full-day Kindergarten program.

After much investigation and speaking with my counter parts in districts that had full-day Kindergarten, I was convinced that it was the way to go. I broached the idea with the Superintendent. First, we determined that each of the six elementary schools could accommodate the additional classrooms that would be needed. Then we discussed the additional cost for doubling the number of Kindergarten teachers. But the State incentive would take care of much of the initial costs. Once we found these concerns could be handled, we discussed the educational ramifications.

We brought the idea to the Board of Education and explained that if full-day Kindergarten was in their future plans they should look into it now. After much discussion considering the State's incentive and the added time for Kindergarteners to prepare for their educational demands, they agreed that now would be a good time to look into it. My charge was to find the benefits and drawbacks of full-day Kindergarten and bring the information to the next board meeting.

I formed a committee made up of the principal, two Kindergarten teachers and two PTA parents from each of the six elementary schools. At our first meeting, the thirty-one of us discussed the issues that were in favor of and against a full-day Kindergarten program. Afterward, each committee member's assignment was to gather every conceivable pro and con question about a full-day program and bring that information to the next meeting.

In the interim, I found six local school districts that already had full-day Kindergarten and asked if they would host a meeting for one of our teams. I explained the makeup of each team and that we would like each member to ask their counterparts the questions that were raised at the meetings. I received agreement from six districts and a morning meeting date was set for the six teams to visit their selected school.

At the second meeting, we compiled the questions that were to be asked by parents, teachers and principals. I explained that they would be visiting school districts that had full-day Kindergarten for some years. Each school was going to set up and host a meeting for them. I told them the date of the meeting. Fortunately, they all could make the time. At the meeting, they were to ask their questions and note the answers. Afterward they would return to the district where we would have lunch and discuss their findings. That was the plan.

The day came and I waited anxiously for the teams to return with their comments. One by one the teams returned and the comments gushed out of them. When we were all together, they began to share their experiences. They were all positive! Even those who were in doubt were convinced after speaking to their counterparts and seeing the children's performance. Changing to Full-Day Kindergarten was even more positive than I hoped.

The committee members attended the next Board meeting and were so upbeat about what they saw that there was hardly any discussion.

Questions asked by those present were easily answered. In every case, the committee members said it would be better for the kids. The Board adopted the plan to begin full-day Kindergarten for the following year.

There is so much to learn it's hard to believe that we ever had half-day.

Chapter 37

My Concern

My Class, My Concern

My first teaching position was a fourth grade class. From day one, I felt that my class and all the children in it were my responsibility. I expected them to learn the material and behave in a manner that would make me proud. That could include the need for me to provide extra help before school began or afterwards for a student who needed it. I would speak to their parents to explain what they could do to help. They were mostly more than willing.

Whatever I did was going to be for the benefit of my charges. So, for example, I went to the audio/visual room and familiarized myself with what was available. I found out that there was money in the budget for A.V. software to go along with the hardware that was hardly used. I perused the fourth grade curriculum and found films and slides that would give my kids another way to learn the curriculum.

I applied for and received permission to take my class on field trips to local places to broaden their experiences. The students wrote and discussed what they had seen and experienced on those trips.

If one of my kids was picked on by another student, I made it my business to inform that student's teacher and we worked together to resolve the problem. If, on a rare occasion, one of my students got into trouble with another teacher or aide, I took it personally. I looked into the situation and talked to that student. We would discuss what had precipitated the issue and how to resolve it. We also discussed the behavior that might have prevented it from becoming an issue. Whatever it took, I was there for my class.

My School, My Concern

After thirteen years as a classroom teacher, I was made Principal of an elementary school. Now my focus changed from a single classroom to the entire school. I must admit that I missed the closeness I had with each of the students in my self-contained class. The one hundred eighty days we spent together gave me the opportunity to really get to know the kids and their families. Now I would be in charge of every aspect of the school. I went from twenty-four students in one classroom, to six hundred students in thirty classrooms. How could I learn all their names? How about the staff? No matter! The same principles would motivate me, except now it would be for the entire school.

I spent most of the first half year getting to know the staff and for the staff to get to know me. I sent a notice to every teacher asking if they had any objection to my eating lunch in their teacher's room. If even one person indicated that they did not wish for me to be in their room, I would not have done so. No one did. In fact, I was welcomed. I ate lunch in their room as often as I could. We spoke about things pertaining to the school as well as those that had nothing to do with school. In that way, we bonded.

During that time, I showed by my actions that I was there to support their efforts. I convinced them that I respected the fact that *they were the ones that "Delivered The Service"* and my job was to help them succeed in that endeavor.

One of the things I had to learn was how to work the system. A good example of that was making up the following year's budget. At the end of my first year, I had some money left in many of the various budgetary categories. For example, I had almost $500 left in my supply budget that had not been spent. I got my first lesson in the way the "System" works when I put in for the $500 that I saved from the previous year's budget. I not only did not get the $500 increase but $500 was deducted from the following year's budget. I was told that since I got along with $500 less this year, I could do with less next year.

I pleaded ignorance and that I was very new to the job and that the school should not suffer due to my ignorance. After a lot of begging I got the $500 put back into the following year's supply budget, but did I learn a lesson? From that year on, I made sure that every penny that was coming to the school was spent before the spending cutoff date. In fact, when the amount was slightly over budget I would put the order in and take the rebuke from the business department.

I would look out more for the school than I even did for myself at home. One time, when I had some money left over that needed to be spent before the deadline, I asked a Kindergarten teacher if there was anything that she needed. She told me she needed an easel. I put the order in and UPS delivered it sometime during the summer.

In September, a few days after school began, the Kindergarten teacher opened the box and found that the easel was broken. I called the company that made the easel and was told that it was past the 30 days I had to report any damages and they were not going to make good. I explained that the easel was delivered during the summer when the teacher was away but as soon as she saw the damage we reported it. "Sorry" the woman on the other end of the phone said, "We have a thirty day policy and you exceeded that time." My response was, "My policy to sign the purchase order for equipment so you can get paid is 90 days. So… if I don't sign for it, you don't get paid. I guess we have to compromise." Long story short we agreed on half the price and the custodian fixed the easel for free.

I was the advocate for my school.

My District, My Concern

When I was appointed Assistant Superintendent, my focus was entirely changed. Now the entire district was my responsibility. I could not become familiar with all the students, teachers and non-teaching personnel in each of the schools.

New building, new office, new secretaries and new jobs were waiting for me. The job was originally listed as Assistant Superintendent for Curriculum K to 6. The job I was hired for was Assistant Superintendent including K-12 Curriculum plus Personnel.

I was very excited about taking on the task of developing a K-12 curriculum.

But instead, my first assignment was to excess 17 tenured teachers due to declining student enrollment. This was an unpleasant experience for me but much more so for those who were going to be without a job. These were good, tenured teachers who had worked in the district for many years. The number of teachers that were to be let go was determined by the contract. The tenure law determined the order of dismissal. The last ones hired by the Board of Education were the first ones to be let go.

There were many ways to inform these teachers of their having to leave. None of them good! I could call them all to a meeting in the Main Office and tell them all at once. I could summon them to my office one at a time and tell them the bad news then or I could have each principal make an appointment for me to meet with each teacher, in their own building and tell them then. I chose the latter. It was the most time consuming for me but I thought best for the teacher. It was meant to show my respect for them.

To go on: Some months later we instituted a remedial math program that needed seven teacher assistants. I immediately thought of the 17 teachers that had been let go. I offered the first seven of them a teacher assistant position. I explained that if they accepted the position it would not affect their return to a permanent position should one become available. The pay was about half of what they had received but it was better than staying home or substituting. The first seven said, "Yes."

Some time later, I had to fill out the B.E.D.S. forms for the state that contained all kinds of information about the district. It included the seven new teacher assistant positions. That brought a phone call from someone at the State Education Department saying these seven were not certified as teacher assistants. "Oh," I explained with gusto, "you don't understand. These seven teacher assistants are fully certified teachers that were let go due to declining enrollment."

"You don't understand," came the answer from the SED person. "They may be certified as teachers but they are not certified as teacher assistants." Can you believe that? I pressed on. "You mean that a fully certified teacher is not automatically certified as a teacher assistant?" "That's correct," said the voice on the other end of the phone. I won't tell you what I said next but suffice it to say it had to do with the intelligence of the people that made this ruling.

After two years as the Assistant Superintendent, I had enough. In addition to being in charge of Curriculum K-12, the Board tacked on "In-Charge-of-Personnel". I was doing ten to twelve hours a day with more bosses, including the nine-member board, less time off and not much more pay. I felt myself burning out.

Having to firing people, dealing with the SED and the nine Board members who, in spite of their lack of experience, each thought they were my boss, made me realize that it was more fun being a school principal.

Fortunately, my wife had the good sense to tell me to take a leave of absence when I left the principal's position. I asked for and was granted a return to being the principal of an elementary school. My request was that I be returned to my old job in my old building. My request was half granted. I would be back as principal, but not of my old building. I was assigned to a building that had a great many problems. I was not happy about not getting back to my old building, but the new assignment certainly became a new challenge.

My New School, My New Concern

The Principal of the school to which I was assigned had just retired. For a long time this school was being considered to be the one to close due to declining student enrollment. As a result, the school building was permitted to deteriorate. The only reason the school was not closed was the persistence of the vocal parents to keep it open.

Window shades were torn and not working. The carpet covering the broken asbestos tiles was worn out. Classrooms had not been painted in years. The hallway flooring needed to be completely replaced. Cafeteria tables were broken. Equipment and supplies were sparse and not updated. All in all, the school was a mess but the parents and teachers were great.

At this time, student enrollment began to increase. No longer was the school being considered for closing. Parents who had been fighting for the school to remain open could now relax, saying they had been right all along. Teachers and custodians were consulted for their input on what was needed. I made a list of what had to be done to bring the school up to where it should be and showed it to the PTA officers. They added things I had not even thought of.

The list was meant to convince everyone that the school was not going to be closed. We agreed that the school had been neglected and needed a great deal of work done as soon as possible. Once the district spent the money to restore the building, there would be no doubt in any parent's mind that the building would remain open.

They were very happy but did not think it could be done. I told them it could!

I showed the extensive list to the Superintendent. He said it was too much to do in one year. I reminded him that the school had been neglected for many years and the monies saved then should be used now to restore the school to where it ought to be. I also told him that I had given the list of upgrades to the PTA officers and that I would hand the list out to the parents attending the first school meeting. They were paying their fair share of taxes all along but not getting their fair share in return. I was sure that the parents who fought to keep the school open were ready to fight for the list of work that needed to be done. The Superintendent reluctantly saw the light and agreed to complete the entire list.

We did two rooms at a time. Two classes were in the cafeteria while painting or floor covering or shades were being upgraded. The school started to shine. It had a positive effect on teachers, students and parents. It seemed that everyone's spirit was lifted as the work was being done. Attendance and grades improved as the building got spruced up! More parents came to PTA meetings to see how their school was being transformed.

It was a good thing!

Chapter 38

New School New Problems

Halloween and Two PTAs

I was preparing my thoughts for assuming the position as the new principal of an old building. One of my mental decisions was to just be an observer for a few months. I didn't want to come into the school like "Gang Busters" and make a lot of changes. The cosmetic changes would be enough. That's a good plan but circumstances got in the way.

The first thing I found was that there were two PTAs. I asked my secretary about this strange setup. She explained that two factions formed over a variety of issues and it was decided to divide into two groups each having different assignments. I would have to learn which PTA was in charge of which activity. I couldn't imagine how but I didn't care. I asked the two PTA presidents to meet with me over lunch in my office, my treat.

After some small talk, I took a deep breath and told them how important I felt a PTA was for a school. I also told them that I was very supportive of PTA in all the years at my previous school. They both said they already knew that from the people they spoke with at a PTA Council meeting.

Now I looked at both of them and said, "I can live with one PTA or no PTA but I can't live with two PTAs. I can't resolve the problems that caused this to happen. Only you two can. So, after lunch I will leave you to resolve the problem. When I return please tell me if we have one PTA or none."

When I returned I was formally introduced to the one and only PTA President. We all shook hands and I told them how happy I was that they resolved what could have been a major problem. The woman who graciously stepped down from office said, "Goodbye" and left. No sooner had I congratulated the new President, then the issue of Halloween came up.

In an effort to provide a safe place for kids to celebrate the holiday, students were invited to the school from 6:00 PM to 8:00 PM on Halloween night. The school's gymnasium and the cafeteria would be the venue. Kids would parade in costume in this safe environment. The PTA ran the show and provided the games and refreshments for the event. It sounded like a good thing.

The evening came and the kids in their costumes came streaming into the building. I noticed that many parents would come to the school, drop their kids off and leave. The PTA volunteers were left to maintain discipline.

I decided that I would be an observer. Unless I saw a potential danger, I would sit back and let the PTA people do their thing. It soon became obvious that the gym and cafeteria were going to be overcrowded. The night custodians stood guard, not letting the kids run through the building. That was good! Some of the kids whose parents dropped them off and left became unruly. The PTA people tried to maintain discipline but were outnumbered and not trained.

PTA had planned a parade for the kids who came in costume. The first to parade was the Kindergarten and their parents. They were the cutest and the best by far. After them came the first grade and their parents. The two parades took a great deal of time. I looked at the clock on the wall. It was 7:30. There was no way that the remaining four grades were going to be able to parade in the next half hour. The PTA noted that too. They tried in vain to organize the four remaining grades into groups that could parade and show off their costumes. The situation was getting tense.

Eight o'clock finally came. Many parents came to pick up their children. I could only imagine how many cars were needed to get the children home. The parking lot was meant for buses, not to accommodate that many cars at the same time. Finding their children and keeping them together as they left was a nightmare. In fact, the whole dismissal was a nightmare.

By 8:30, a dozen or so people were left to watch the kids of the parents who were late getting back to the school to pick up their children. I thanked the people who remained and told them that I would wait with the remaining kids and they should take their own children and go home. They were very thankful!

A week later, I met with the PTA people that ran the Halloween event. I asked if what happened was typical of past Halloween events. They sheepishly said it was always the same. We discussed the negative aspects of the event and how best to resolve the problems that came with this good deed. There seemed to be no way to resolve the problems other than to cancel the event. That's what was decided!

Good or bad, the principal sets the tone for the school.

Chapter 39

Elective Mute

The school year had begun and routines were in place. My plan was not to make changes right away. I had to establish myself as the Principal of the school and I knew all eyes were watching to see how I would lead. Shortly after I became Principal, I became aware of a new problem.

One day just after lunch, a third grade teacher became ill. There was only a little more than an hour left before dismissal. It was too late to call for a substitute and I never wanted to disrupt the other classes of the grade by dividing the students into their classes. I decided to cover the class for the remainder of the day. First it would send a message to the staff that I was still a teacher and second it would give me the opportunity to get to know some of the kids and for them to get to know me.

I came to the room and found the teacher sitting with a reading group. I told her I would take the class and that she could go home. She was very grateful. She gave me some quick instructions for what I would have to do and left.

I sat down and began calling on the kids one at a time. I asked them to tell me their name and then to read a paragraph or two from their reading book. As each finished I thanked them and went on to the next student. I came to the next student, a girl who just stared at me when I asked for her name. I waited a few seconds but got no response. Another student in the group spoke up and said, "She doesn't speak." I said, "Okay" and went on to the next child. I couldn't wait to get back to the office to find out about this.

After dismissal, I rushed back to the office and asked my secretary what she knew about this girl. In a nonchalant voice, she told me that she had never spoken in school. I couldn't believe what followed. It seems that she had not spoken a single word in school for the more than three years. Not one word! How could that be?

I checked her records. Her grades were all A or B. There was a record of some parent conferences where it was agreed that she was "Quiet"! The school psychologist was involved and it was decided that this little girl didn't have to speak until she was ready. In fact, anytime she felt pressured to speak she would get very upset. She passed all her written tests and didn't cause any trouble in class. I was appalled!

I spoke to a number of professionals and described the girl's behavior. They all told me I was dealing with an elective mute and the symptoms I described were serious. They couldn't believe that the condition had gone on for so long with nothing being done about it. Neither could I. I spoke to every one of the teachers that had anything to do with the girl from Kindergarten to the current grade and was told that the school psychologist had advised that they not pressure the child into talking. She said something like, "When she is ready she will talk." Well she hadn't!

Next, I spoke to Steve, the district's social worker, and explained what I had heard from the teachers. We agreed that we had to start from scratch and pursue the issue. Once we felt prepared with the facts, we set up an appointment with the parents of this girl.

On the appointed day, only the mother arrived. She was very defensive. She told us that this situation had been resolved with the previous principal and psychologist and she hoped I would understand and leave things alone. We tried to convince her that this was a serious problem that needed professional help. She did not agree. She just kept repeating that the girl spoke at home and was very shy only in school. Try as we might, we could not convince the mother that this should not go on.

After the meeting, Steve and I discussed the options available to us. He asked if he could try to work with the parent and the girl in a very gentle way to see if he could bring about a change. I agreed to let him try for a while.

At that time, the Cabbage Patch Doll was very popular. It was so popular that all the stores ran out of them. The more difficult they became to find, the more they were sought after. Somehow, Steve got hold of one. He was going to use it to bribe the girl into speaking.

Steve met with her and showed her the doll. The girl's eyes lit up. He told her that all she had to do was to say, "I would like to have that doll. Could I please have it?" and it would be hers. The battle between wanting that doll and keeping silent must have raged in the girl's head. She wanted that doll very much! But in the final analysis, she did not speak. Steve tried many different ways but they all failed to get her to talk.

We finally decided to bring the matter to the Committee On the Handicapped. (COH). The first problem was that her grades were too good for making the case. Her grades were all A or B. Not the grades of someone who has learning problems.

Steve and I spoke to the classroom teacher and we agreed that she would ask the girl to read at the next reading group meeting. If she refused, she was to be given a zero for that lesson. The same would be for all the other academic subjects. Each time she was asked a question and did not answer, she would get a zero.

The grades on her next report card went from A and B to F. Now I could bring the issue to the COH. After many difficulties it was determined that this was a seriously disabling problem and a special class for emotionally disturbed children would be the best placement for her. The parent was informed of the decision and surprisingly did not object.

The next day she was transferred to the building that housed that class. The principal and teachers of the school were advised of the problem. The following day the Principal called me and said, "What are you talking about? The girl is speaking in class! She is reading in her group and answering questions in the other subjects." At first, I thought he was kidding but he was serious. She was really speaking in class! She was still being an elective mute, but now she elected not to be mute!

It seems that the girl was so invested in her silence at our school that she was unable to speak for fear of the attention that would befall her. However, when she got to the new school she had the opportunity to break her silence and did so.

The principal is sometimes the child's main advocate.

Chapter 40

Speaking

The Curriculum Vs. Life's Needs

We spend a lot of time in school teaching children to listen! "Pay attention to what I say." It begins in Kindergarten and increases all the way to college where we listen to lectures in large Lecture Halls and say nothing. We listen so we can answer questions given on tests about things we listened to. We memorize facts so that we can pass written tests. Some of us even do some creative writing but we seldom speak and even when we do it is to answer a specific question posed by our teachers.

Conversely, as adults we are asked to do a lot of speaking. We speak to friends, relatives, fellow employees, doctors, therapists, clients, bosses, professionals and others. We speak face to face or on the telephone. When we have a thought to convey we generally speak to the person or persons who we want to hear it. Yet, we continue to train students to listen but not how to ask questions, carry on conversations, or speak in public.

It sounds to me like we are doing things backwards in schools. Instead of focusing teaching on how to convey information through speech, we stress listening and the recalling of facts for written tests. Since students and their teachers are evaluated on the results of these written tests, there is little need to stress or teach speaking. As a result, the shy student who sits quietly in class and contributes very little verbally can receive good grades.

Many children sit in the back of the classroom hoping never to be called upon to speak. New teachers often fall into the trap of calling on the same few hand raising students who like to speak out while the ones who would like never to answer questions are happy to be left alone. As a result, shy turns into fear for many of them.

A college friend of mine told me he had an interview for a job coming up in less than a week and he was "scared to death". When I asked him why, he told me that he always 'freaks' at interviews. He admitted that he always sat in the back of the room and hoped the teacher would not call on him and, for the most part, they didn't. But now someone was going to ask him questions directly and he had to answer them. That he did well at the interview was very important for his getting the job. The pressure he put on himself was adding to his fears. He asked if I could help.

First, I had him interview himself. He was to write down every conceivable question he thought his interviewer could ask. Then he was to set up a tape recorder and record each question. Once he had the questions, he was to sit in front of a mirror and answer each taped question, recording the whole session. I told him to look at the expression on his face as he answered the questions. Where necessary he should smile. At other times, he should be serious. Sometimes he should pause and other times he should answer quickly. When finished, I told him to listen to his interview and evaluate each of his responses. He could change those that needed to be fixed.

We then talked about how he should dress and look. We spoke about how important eye contact is. We worked on his voice so it was firm and clear. I told him to look up the company and find areas where his skills match their needs. I then convinced him that he knew more about himself than his interviewer knew of him and the job was right for him. He set about practicing what we had discussed. When he thought he had done it enough times, I interviewed him. Long story short, he got the job!

Chapter 41

The TLC Card

Some Kids Really Need One. So Do Some Adults

Speaking of Tender Love and Care…Too often, children come to school with the weight of the world on their small shoulders. A death in the family or the throws of a parental divorce can have a devastating affect on a child.

Whenever I learned about something like this happening to a child, I would send a note to all the teachers and staff and ask them to go out of their way to make this child feel good about themselves. I didn't have to explain the reason; they knew it was for something important.

One particular situation stands out in my mind. One early December day, a very nicely dressed couple came to my office. They had two daughters who attended our school. One was eight in the third grade and the other was ten and in the fifth grade. The couple explained in a very articulate manner that they were about to be divorced and they chose to wait until after Christmas to tell their children. This was so the children could enjoy the holiday. I must say this seemed very strange to me. In all other divorce cases I had come across, the couples were barely speaking to each other. These two seemed very friendly. But I kept a straight face and just listened.

They went on to tell me that they were both distressed over how the girls might react once they knew about their plan to split. They were both concerned for their daughters' welfare and wanted the school to know about it and do what we could to mitigate any problems. This was going to be a very different divorce. The couple was so amicable in relating their concerns to me that I had all I could do not to ask them why they had decided to split. I assured them that I would keep a special eye on the kids and let them know if their teachers saw any change in their behavior or their studies.

After they left, I sent a note to every staff member who had any dealings with the two girls asking for a quick evaluation of their behavior and academics.

The staff was used to getting requests from me asking for a thumbnail sketch for a student who was having trouble of some sort or other. This time, each return asked why I had asked about these two children "They are both well adjusted, top students who are liked by their peers and teachers," was the typical response. I placed the responses in an envelope marked "Open at the end of January".

Four weeks after the divorce I sent the same request to the staff. This time the responses were very different. "What happened?" "She used to be so happy and bubbly." "She doesn't smile anymore and failed a math test." The rest of the returned notes were all written in the same vein for both girls.

I made it my business to speak to each of the girls. They were both reticent to speak at first but after a bit of questioning about their grades, they opened up to me and said they could not understand why their parents had to divorce? "They didn't hate each other like my friends' parents who divorced." "They didn't even fight!" What had they done to cause this was their question. I made it clear that they had nothing to do with the divorce and that I knew that both their parents loved both of them.

I called the parents and shared with them the returned notes from the teachers. They were both very taken aback by the reports. "We tried so hard to do this the right way," they both lamented. "Did we make a mistake?" The best I could say was to recommend they get some counseling for both themselves and the girls.

It left me with the question. Is it better for the kids to see their parents fighting with each other so they have some reason for why they split?

Maybe there is no right way!

The School Phobic & Visualization

When I was in the 6ᵗʰ grade, I had a teacher who was very strict and picked on a few of the boys, me among them. I didn't know how to deal with it. After a while, I did not want to go to school. I started feeling nauseous every morning.

Of course, my mother told me not to be so sensitive and made sure I went to school. Little by little, I felt worse. The more I tried not to think about the nausea the worse it got. It got so bad that my mother took me to a doctor. He gave me some medicine to take that didn't work. My mother tried telling me it would go away once I got to school. But it didn't! Then she became angry with me and told me to stop acting like a baby. The angrier she got, the worse the nausea became. I hated being yelled at but more than that, I hated myself. I had no control over my problem and it was getting worse!

As time progressed, the nausea increased and would come over me every time I left the house. I had become a full-blown phobic but I didn't know what that was. The summer came and school finally ended but my problem persisted. My world was shrinking.

My father's boss lived in Great Neck, Long Island. Every summer he invited all his workers and their families to his house for a picnic. I was frightened about going but had no choice. I started feeling nauseous as soon as we left the apartment. How was I going to get through this without my nausea taking over? How helpless did I feel?

When we got there, I met his three sons who were around my age. They were going to ride their bikes and asked me to join them. How was I going to be able to hide my problem from them? I told them that I had never ridden a two-wheeled bike before. We lived on the top floor of a walkup apartment so there was no way I could own a bike. It looked like fun but also very scary. I couldn't imagine how it could stay upright. They told me it was easy and gave me a bike to ride. They made it sound so easy that I couldn't say "no". "Just get on the bike, peddle fast and it will stay up."

I was so afraid of riding the bike that I forgot about being nauseous. I got on the bike and began peddling. It was downhill so there was no problem going fast. Amazingly, the bike remained upright. What a great feeling I was having! It got better and better as I picked up speed. This was the greatest! I was riding a two-wheeled bike for the first time and doing it well! I was so proud of myself.

They hadn't told me how to stop, but that's another story. I finally, after so many months, had a reason to feel good about myself! Even my nausea was gone for the moment! It was as if I was a new person. I thought I was cured. But when I got home the nausea returned. This time I thought about how good I felt while riding the bike and the nausea went away. Could I control the nausea by getting myself to visualize riding the bike? Yes! It worked! All I had to do was to concentrate on the wonderful feelings I experienced that first time riding down the hill and the nausea would go away. I could finally control the problem! That may have been the best day of my life!

I used that visualization technique many times. Each time I was able to control the phobic feelings that used to plague me. In September I returned to school with the knowledge that if I started to get those feelings all I had to do was visualize riding that bike and the feelings would go away. I was in control not the fear!

Years went by and I was sitting at my desk when the intercom called me to attention. My secretary told me there was a parent on the phone who wanted to speak with me. When she got on, she began to cry. She told me that her son had become a "School Phobic" and she didn't know whom to blame. I settled her down and asked her if she could get her son to school. "Just bring him to my office". She said she would try and was able to do so. When they arrived, I asked her to wait outside and let me talk to her son alone. She reluctantly did.

I could see the same look of fear in his eyes that I had experienced so many years before. I began by telling him of my phobic experiences when I was about his age. I told him that what I was about to tell him was between us. Telling him that I had the same experience and that I knew how to show him how to fix it got his attention. He listened to my story and began to relax a bit.

I told him about that wonderful day in my life when I rode a two-wheeled bicycle for the first time and how it made me feel. I went on to tell him of my visualization method that I used and how it worked for me. I told him that I could teach him how to do it and he would be able to control his fears. Control, not stop, was the key word. He often tried to stop his fears but he couldn't. Other people tried to tell him to stop his fears but he couldn't. I was going to show him how to "control" his fear. I was winning his confidence.

I began by asking him to close his eyes and describe to me the best incident he could ever remember that happened to him. It took a while and some coaxing but we finally arrived at a time when he hit a home run and his teammates all congratulated him as he crossed home plate.

I then had him reenact that scene in his mind in minute detail. With his eyes closed, I had him set the scene. It was a warm, sunny day with a slight breeze blowing out toward center field. He described seeing the ball leave the pitcher's hand. Then the feeling in his muscles as he gripped the bat and got ready to swing. Feeling the swing as he stepped into the oncoming ball. He could hear the sound of the bat hitting the ball and then followed the trajectory of the ball as it flew over the outfielder's head.

Now I had him mentally run the bases touching each one as it came up. Feeling his foot as it touched each base. He realized this was going to be an extra base hit. As he rounded second, he looked over his right shoulder and saw that the outfielder had just gotten to the ball. He rounded third and raced for home. He slid into home plate and heard the umpire's call, "Safe." He hit a homer!

He heard the cheers and felt the smile on his face. He saw his parents standing among the other spectators and cheering as loud as ever they had. "How good did you feel at that moment?" I asked. As he did this, he noticed that he felt pretty good while relating the scene.

He realized that he did not feel the fear while describing the event. I told him to go home and practice that scene repeatedly and to use it exactly that way any time he felt his fear coming on. "Don't let the fear beat you! Control it!"

Weeks later his Mom sent me a letter that read, "I don't know what you told him and he will not tell me, but he is a changed child. Thank you." I cherish that letter.

Everything you learn in life can be of value in helping others.

Chapter 42

Collegial Circles

Getting One Started

A collegial circle involves a group of people who have common interests and are willing to share their knowledge and experience with people who have similar interests.

The Benefits:

Teachers and administrators live in a very small world with big world problems. They have very little time to share their problems with others who very often are coping with the same problems. An interchange of ideas can often lead to appropriate solutions. Even if they don't, it is helpful knowing that others in their position have to deal with the same problems. Best of all it gives people an opportunity to focus on a single problem.

Membership:

New teachers, senior teachers, new principals & senior principals could all benefit from a collegial circle. People new to the job can hear how "old timers" handled similar situations. People who have been on the job for many years can benefit from a fresh way to look at a problem. In short, everyone can benefit from the mix.

Guidelines:

A collegial circle is an ongoing operation that needs a commitment of time and responsibility. Every effort must be made to attend the regular meetings. While attending, members must contribute as well as listen. Which brings me to the issue of "confidentiality". What is said in the group stays in the group unless the group agrees to pass it on. People must know that what they say is respected even if disagreed with.

Getting Started:

Talk it up! People interested in starting a collegial circle should start talking about the idea to people who share their interests and concerns. These can be people from within their school, in their district or even from other districts. The benefits and the commitments to time should be made clear. Once there are four or more people who have shown an interest, choose a time and place to begin the process.

Sharing:

It is important for the participants to get to know each other and that should begin at the first meeting. A good icebreaker is something called "two truths and a lie". This is where each person chooses two interesting or important things that really happened in their life and one lie that sounds believable. Each person then reads their three statements and it is up to the group to guess which one is the lie. You will be amazed at how much you will learn about each person.

The Topic for Discussion:

Start with a brainstorming session with the idea of making a list of issues that the circle should consider. List every idea that is offered. Combine those that are similar. Select a topic that seems to have the greatest interest with the knowledge that the other issues will be discussed at future meetings.

Setting the Next Meeting:

Everyone needs to know the what, where and when of the next meeting. A topic should be selected so that each can think about it in advance of the meeting.

The Central Team:

The "central team" is made up of 4 positions that should be designated at the end of each meeting along with knowing their responsibilities:

*The Host; provides the place, refreshments and sends a reminder invitation.

*The Facilitator; keeps people on task during the meeting and announces the next topic as determined by the group.

*The Recorder; takes notes of the meeting and sends them via E-Mail or snail mail to all the members. These notes are kept in a loose-leaf notebook and passed on to the next recorder. It should contain the "Best Practices" of the discussions.

*The Researcher; is responsible for getting information about the topic and distributing that to the members days before the meeting. Other members of the group are encouraged to share their research with the researcher.

Keep the Circle Going Around.

Chapter 43

The Principal, Teacher, Mentor

The Mind Reading Trick

Young children are particularly vulnerable to the hucksters that they see on television or on computers who hawk merchandize or ideas meant to excite them. They beg their parents to buy things for them because they look or sound so good. Some turn out to be what they say but many are fraudulent and disappointing. People today are bombarded with information that is sometimes accurate and unfortunately sometimes inaccurate. This lesson is meant to teach children to be critical of what they hear and see because they can easily be fooled. The following lesson has to do with perception and misperception.

I start by asking a classroom teacher if they would like me to teach a lesson to their class. The lesson is meant to teach the kids how easily they can be fooled by what is said on TV or on computers. The response is almost always "Yes". Teachers love to see the Principal teach a lesson.

The lesson is called, "Communication". It utilizes a "mind reading" trick that goes like this: I introduce the lesson to the class by talking about how various ideas and thoughts can be transmitted from one person to another. Students are asked to contribute examples. The most common answers are computers, radio, television, telephone, person to person, teacher to students and so on. When we run out of ways and if it has not been suggested, I bring up "ESP" and "mind reading".

We talk about extra sensory perception (ESP) and what that means. I spend some time getting a little argument going between those who believe in ESP and those who don't. Some good stories often come out of that discussion. I ask the students if they think people can read the minds of others? A few say "yes", most say "no". "Well, let's find out." I say, "I sense that someone in this class can read my mind." I then proceed with the trick.

How it works:

Days before the lesson I ask the teacher to give me the name of a student who is usually not included in group activities. I want the one who is chosen last when the leaders choose sides for anything. Very often, this is a shy girl who the other girls have left out of their inner circle. I certainly would not choose the most popular student of the class. Teachers know who that child is and are very interested in selecting them. In this case, it was a girl.

Armed with the name I find a time when I can secretly talk to the youngster. I ask her if she is interested in helping me with a lesson that I will teach her class. The answer is always "Yes."

I tell her that the lesson is designed to fool the members of her class into believing something that their logic tells them is not possible but their eyes and ears tell them otherwise. This is meant to peak her interest. After promising to keep the secret, I tell her how the trick works. I also tell her she will have to be a very good actor to make it work. Everybody wants to be a good actor!

I explain that I will come to her class tomorrow and begin by talking about many things but eventually I will get to the real topic, which is ESP (Extra Sensory Perception). I will then ask those in the class to raise their hand if they believe some people have the ability to read minds. You will timidly raise your hand. Then I will ask those who do not believe it to raise their hand.

Next I will say that somehow I get the feeling that someone in this class can read my mind. I will then spend some time building the suspense. Finally, I will ask if they would like to see if maybe someone in the class is able to read my mind. They always say "yes." Then I will pause and say, "Tell you what, I'll choose a number from 0 to 500, write it down and concentrate on that number to see if any student receives a 'Telepathic' message with the correct number". Of course, my secret assistant, you will know in advance the number that I will choose. The number is 246; please remember it.

When the time comes I will carefully write the secret number, "246" down on a piece of paper making sure that no one can see what I write. Then I will appear to strongly concentrate on that number and ask each student to write any number that comes to their mind on their piece of paper. After concentrating very hard, and all writing seems to have been completed, I will ask everyone to hold up the paper containing their number. Of course my secret assistant, you will hold up the correct number "246". If someone else guesses the right number, I will ask both to continue but that has never happened.

When you hold up your paper with the number "246" on it I will say, 'Wow'! With great fanfare, I will show the class that I had written the number 246! I will go on to say, "That was great!" and pointing to you, "Do you think you can read my mind?" You answer in a timid voice, "maybe." I will say, "Let's try it with objects in the room."

I will explain to the class that you will leave the room. While you are out of sight and hearing, someone in the class will choose an object that is somewhere in the classroom.

You will then be called back into the room. I will tell you that I will concentrate on an object in the room. You too will concentrate as you try to read my mind. I will then point to various objects around the classroom such as the door or a desk and ask you if that is what you see in your mind? You will take your time, concentrate very hard and finally say "no" to each one.

After you reject 4 or 5 items, I will point to something that has the color red anywhere in it. For example, the flag or a painting that has any red color in it. You will take your time but finally say "no."

The very next object I point to will be the one the class chose! Remember, object chosen by the class is the one just <u>after</u> the one that contained any red color. That will be the next one that I point to!

I will ask in the same voice "Is it...?" And I will point to the object selected.

You will take your time thinking and sheepishly say "yes." This is sure to get gasps from the class and I will play it up.

We will do this two or three more times using different objects and different methods including no voice, just pointing. You of course will choose the one that comes just after the object that has some red color. I will make a bigger fuss after each attempt. Finally, I will ask the class how many have changed their mind about ESP and mind reading. Most, if not all, hands will go up.

I then will introduce you as my assistant and tell the class that they have been tricked and you were in on the trick. We will talk about how easily they were fooled, but I will not tell them how it is done nor should you. This is the magician's secret.

I do one or two rehearsals with my assistant to be sure she got the entire trick right and we shake hands and part. We did the trick the next day and it was great! It always is. This is a great lesson for many reasons but mainly to teach critical thinking.

Looking is not always seeing!

Chapter 44

This Is What It's All About

At the end of my first year as a teacher, I received my first notes from parents of my students thanking me for being their child's teacher. They were wonderful and treasured. I decided to empty a drawer in my desk and save them.

Through the years I cherished the fact that someone took the time to write a note thanking me for what I had done for his or her child. Some were particularly gratifying. Year after year I saved these letters and read them all at the end of each school year.

As I write this, I wonder how many of my own teachers knew what a profound effect they had on my life.

I think of Mr. Edmond Morton, my unofficial guidance counselor at Manual Training High school. Mr. Morton always knew when to be tough and when to be gentle. For the entire four years of High School, he took a personal interest in all of us in his homeroom. I can still hear him saying, when we were not living up to his standards, "You sons of guns and I don't mean guns." This coming from the most proper teacher I ever knew. I wonder if he knew how much his words shaped my behavior. Did he realize that I tried even harder so as not to disappoint him?

Then there was Dr. Sherwig, the best teacher I ever had at New Paltz State University. He was known to be the toughest marker and the best lecturer in the school. As tough a marker as he was I still took every class he taught. It was not too good for my grade average but he was great for what I learned. I can still hear his voice as he lectured about the battle of Gettysburg. The class sat in awe as he

251

moved toward the door saying his last sentence. "Blood from both sides mingled on the battlefield". Then he opened the door and left. None of us moved for what seemed like a long time. He brought history to life. He also knew how to motivate for excellence. Did he know that I felt that way about him? I hope so because he deserved to know.

Mr. Helmer Peterson was the district Superintendent for West Babylon. At every welcome back meeting in September, he made the same speech to the entire staff. I can still hear his magical words. "You as teachers are dealing with the most precious possession parents have. They would give up everything they own but keep their children." How simple, important and honest his words were. I hope in addition to me, people told him how much of an impression it made on the staff!

Educators frequently do not know how or when they have influenced the lives of their charges. It is a special gift when they are told.

When I was about to retire I looked at the hundreds of letters stored in my top draw and realized that I was going to begin a new life in retirement. I decided to read them one more time and then discard them. They all brought back wonderful memories and it became harder and harder to discard them. At last, I decided to keep about 50 of them. It is fitting that the last chapter of this book should contain excerpts from letters I received from a teacher, a parent and students.

Letter from a teacher: 9/30/94

Dear Mr. Schiffman,

I needed to let you know the enormous impact that you have had on my life.

You came into my life on 3 separate occasions each time influencing me in a very positive way. The first time that you entered my life I was 10 years old. You opened up a "world of learning without boundaries". You allowed me to explore and discover. You started the spark that ignited my "love of learning". The second time that you came into my life was at my 1969 H.S. graduation. I'll never forget the disappointment in your eyes when I told you that I would not be attending college. I also never forgot your words: "you can be the best at whatever you choose to do." Those words remained with me and were the spark that ignited my pursuit of becoming a teacher.

And the third time that you entered my life was in September 1989, twenty years after my H.S. graduation. I'll never forget the look in your eyes when I told you that I was subbing that day in your school. It was quite different from the look that I saw 20 years prior. And when I became your fifth-grade teacher, our circle was complete.

You are very special to me in so many ways, teacher, mentor, friend. There will always be a very special place in my heart for you.

With All My Love,

Susan

Letter from a parent: 4/24/85

Dear Mr. Schiffman,

I felt it was necessary to write you a note thanking you for the way you helped me handle my recent problem. In all the years I have been involved with this school I have never received such warm and compassionate understanding.

I also feel I must tell you that this year I have seen many wonderful changes in our school and I thank you for them.

My only regret is I will not have a child in your school next year, but I am looking forward to the following year when my next one starts Kindergarten.

Thank you

Mrs. Sue Drago

Letter from a student: 9/29/94

Dear Mr. Schiffman

Yesterday when we had the concert it made me, Christina and Jamie cry so much that our faces were beet red. We are really sad that you are leaving. We wish that you would retire when we are in junior high school so we can have memories of 4th and 5th grade. When you leave the school totally, I'm going to make believe that you are still here. We really can't wait until we see you again in the school. But we will still have the memories of you as our principal.

Love, Kimberly Marie Capasso

A student in your school

Letter from a student: 6/20/86

Dear Mr. Schiffman

You saved my life. I was afraid to go to school and you taught me how to think of hitting a home run whenever I started to feel afraid. I am still afraid but I think of what you told me and it goes away.

Thanks,

Your student William

Chapter 45

Fix The Problems

Ask Those Who Never Taught? I think NOT!

I thought I had finished writing this book when a friend who had just finished reading it asked accusingly, "What would you do to fix it?" I thought about it and decided the book needed another chapter. I realize that it may be presumptuous of me to think I could fix the long-standing problems facing education today with a chapter in this book but certain problems stand out. For too long "more of the same" has been the fix. "No Child Left Behind" sounded good but was doomed to failure before it got started. "Reach For The Stars" will meet with the same failing results. At best, they treat the symptoms not the causes. So here goes:

1. Have teachers administer a Standardized test in early September and do an "item analyses" of the results. Using the results, teachers can find out what learning problems need fixing. They can begin correcting these learning gaps early. If at the end of a reasonable period of time there is no improvement for some students, teachers can seek help. Fixing the problem may mean short time remediation by teachers that specialize in that student's problem or help for that teacher's problem. It is a bad idea to allow a learning gap to persist.

2. Conversely, do not use a Standardized Test at the end of the school year to test students! That only tests teachers and the more pressure put on teachers for their class to score high on that test the more time they will spend gearing their lessons toward, "Teaching To The Test". Often that produces what I call, "Legal or even illegal cheating". Legal cheating is preparing students for taking the test by encouraging them to "Guess." "Guess when you can eliminate even one of the four answers you are given to choose from. An answer left blank is counted as wrong anyway, so guess!"

The odds of getting a correct answer do go up as you can eliminate wrong answers but does that mean the student knows the information? "No!" It means they learned how to play the odds. Good maybe for Vegas but not for learning.

Another method for legal cheating is to look at previous tests and select the vocabulary or the examples that come up most frequently. Drill those words even though they may not be the vocabulary students need to know in order to write better.

What I call illegal cheating ranges from giving more time to take the test than indicated on the instructions or worse, walking around the room telling students to, "Take another look at #6." The worst is when some, very few, change incorrect answers to correct ones when grading them.

Illegal cheating will escalate when Merit Pay or Job Security is added to the mix! That's a no-brainer! So let's look at what goes into constructing a standardized test.

A standardized test by its very nature must be:

a. Easy to administer: Students are given a booklet of questions where the answers are true/false, fill in the blanks or choose from a b c or d.

b. Easy to score: Students are given an answer sheet where they using a #2 pencil, fill in a bubble for what they consider to be the correct answer. An answer sheet overlay is then used to find correct answers and grade the test. Simple!

c. Easily disseminated: Scores can be disaggregated so as to report results to the local public, the SED and newspapers.

Note: The time taken to prepare for the test always takes time away from creativity, the teachable moment and other important learning.

3. Increase the school year to 230 days from the 180 that is now required for students and teachers. Counting the 104 weekend days, that still leaves 31 days for vacations and holidays. The idea for not having school from the end of June to the beginning of September so that kids can work on the farm is antiquated. If you ever taught you know how much time a teacher must take each September catching the kids up to what was forgotten during those 10 summer weeks.

Add 50% to the teacher's salary. The prospect of working 230 days for a good salary will attract a different work force. They will not have to work as camp counselors or waiters in the summer. They will be "Full Time Teachers"! Students will have 50 more days to compete in the computer world in which they will live.

To those who question what will become of camps and vacation places, I was asked to fix schools not vacations. By the way, air-condition all schools where summer temperatures reach over 75 degrees. Kids and teachers live in air-conditioned environments and are not used to classrooms that get unbearably hot during the summer months.

In the beginning, this plan should be a voluntary choice for students and teachers. Those teachers who choose to take on the additional days of school will be compensated for their extra time sufficiently so as to motivate other teachers to do the same. These volunteers will be experienced teachers selected on the basis of their past performance. The curriculum for students will be changed to accommodate the 50 additional days. Problem solving will be emphasized using the skills concomitant with Project Based Learning Units (PBLU). (See Chapters 3 & 9) In time, all schools will change to 230 days and the additional cost will be well worth it.

4. Project Based Learning Units (PBLU) will be infused into the curriculum and required activities during the school year. Teachers will teach students "How To Learn" and give them the tools necessary to accomplish the required tasks. Isolated, memorized facts, whose sole purpose is to rate teacher and student performance on a short answer test will be kept to a minimum or eliminated when proven to be of little value. The current student lives in the computer age where facts are readily available. It is more important to teach students how to retrieve and determine the reliability of the information. When the purpose is to improve memory have students memorize a poem or the Preamble of the Constitution.

The number of Project Based Learning Unit segments will be determined by grade level. For example but not limited to: one for grades K&1, two for grades 2 to 4, three for grades 5 to 7 and four for grades 8 to12. These units will play a major roll in the evaluation system that will be used to determine each student's progress. (See chapter 5 of this book for more details).

5. Begin Kindergarten for boys 6 months later than girls. It is common knowledge that five year-old girls are more verbal than five-year boys. That means girls experience success sooner than boys. Beginning school with a built in deficit can often produce a feeling of failure. This can be a hindrance to future learning.

Those of us who realize this often advise parents to hold off registering boys born near the Kindergarten cutoff date. Some agree, some don't. It has been my experience that those who agree do not regret the decision.

6. Fix the colleges that teach teachers how to teach. College education teachers must have taught at the grade levels they teach about for at least 5 years before they can teach prospective teachers or principals how to perform their duties. That goes for members of the State Education Department, school administrators and post-graduate education professors. Before they can be involved in making any educational decisions, they must have recently experienced teaching in a classroom. It is too easy to minimize problems after a few years of being out of the classroom. I was taking a class at NYU when the professor tapped his pen on the desk to get order. Everyone stopped talking and were ready to listen. I told the professor in most schools he could tap his pen on the desk till it went all the way through and not get order.

Things change today at a more accelerated rate than ever before. The tools for learning and the curriculum must be able to change with the times. What worked 30 years ago when there were no personal computers, and iPads, and Twitter to name a few, will not work today. The thinking of people based on their personal school experience is of questionable value and inhibits change.

7. Most teachers would agree that the best learning that they experienced for becoming a teacher occurred during their student-teaching time. So…

  a.' Increase the student/teacher experience to two full years. The first year should be as an observer/teacher, teaching a single lesson critiqued by their Master Teacher. The second year they should be considered interns where they are responsible for various parts of the day and curriculum.

  b. Since there is little involvement by the college during this period the majority of the tuition collected by the college should be divided between the master-teacher who is training the student and the intern.

  c. Have the State pay for 90% of every basic education budget with local communities adding at least 10% to make it 100%. Local Boards Of Education may increase that 10% if they so desire by a public referendum.

   d. All new rulings mandated by the State or Federal government will be fully paid for by the State or the Fed that issued it. The payment will continue for as long as the mandate is in affect.

8. Have people with teaching experience make the rules for teaching. Keep politicians and business people out of the teaching part of the curriculum. People who have no more knowledge about teaching a student than their own school experience should not determine how teachers teach.

Teaching children is not like selling cars or making widgets. Each learner is different. Those differences are evident even before they come to Kindergarten. There are tall ones and short ones, shy ones or outspoken ones, those who are verbal and those who are not and they all come from different backgrounds just to name a few. We even see major differences within families. Siblings are different from their siblings. There are countless differences and combinations of these in five-year olds.

The differences get greater as they get older. Unlike making the exact same item countless times, measuring student progress is far more complicated. No Single Test Can Measure That! Nor should it.

9. Parents play an important roll in their child's education and should be encouraged to attend evening meetings, sponsored by the school to find out what they can do to assist the teacher. Parents want their children to succeed in school, but many do not know how or what their roll should be. This can be embarrassing.

"Meet The Teacher Night" which is usually one hour in length, is nowhere near enough time. The parent leaves with little more knowledge for what they can do to help their child than they had to start. With more time, teachers could explain the curriculum for the year and give parents specific ways for them to become actively involved in their student's learning.

10. Teachers must be in contact with parents frequently during the school year. The typical report card that is sent home 3 or 4 times a year has been of little use and misinterpreted for decades. For example, what does the letter C on a report card mean? Does C indicate average performance? Is it given based on how hard the student tried? Is it how much of the subject they know? Or is it a combination of the two? Sometime the only beneficiary is the economy when an "A" is rewarded with money.

We have all experienced having had "Hard Markers" and "Easy Markers" in school. Should parents factor that into the report card grade? I turned the same term paper into two different professors and got two different grades. Have you? With today's variety of communication methods such as Cell Phones, Texting, Snail Mail and Email, reporting progress can and should be often and a two way street. Teachers and parents can call, text or email each other with information that can help their student learn.

11. Teacher and student evaluation:

  a. by the principal's observations. There are a variety of ways to observe a lesson that will help a teacher learn how they can improve. The principal should be familiar with all of them. The observation itself must be a collaborative experience in order to be helpful.

  b. Keep test results and written material in each student's folder to be used for evaluating progress. Teachers and students should periodically review the material.

  c. Grade each student's oral presentation according to preset conditions that are known to the student. That should be part of the evaluation process.

  d. Tests, both grade-level and teacher-made, should be given and corrected often. Teachers and pupils should review the results of the test so as to correct mistakes before they become entrenched.

e. Include the results of the item analysis of a Standardized Test given in September in each student's folder. The test results should be used to give the teacher an indication of the student's learning level for various subject areas. Discuss individual goals with the student to determine what progress can be expected. This becomes part of the teacher/student evaluation process.

12. The principal's job

There are many remedies for fixing teaching problems ranging from reading an article to taking additional courses at a college. Setting up a fellow-teacher observation day, is often very helpful. There are many others.

New teachers come to their first year of teaching with lots of enthusiasm but very little experience. Teaching is far more difficult than many new teachers realize. Poor disciplinary control is often the symptom and main cause for a teacher's failure. A few teachers come to the profession with what I call "The Magic" but most need direction and time to become successful. They have spent time, effort and money getting their degree and certification. They are entitled to help in correcting problems.

Ignore the criticisms that are hurled at teachers like tenure, short hours and 40 weeks. Those same criticisms have been around since before I started teaching in 1952. People were lamenting then how good times used to be. Non-teachers thought they knew then what the right way was to teach, as they claim to know now. They were wrong then and they are wrong now.

Not everyone is meant to be a teacher! If, after many attempts to correct serious problems they persist, it may be time to tell the teacher to look for a different profession. NYS law gives the principal 3 years to make a recommendation before tenure may be granted. It is never easy to tell someone that they are not cut out to be a teacher but in the long run it can be best for them, the students and the school. It is very hard and upsetting to come to school each day knowing you can't control and teach your class!

With regard to tenure: There was a time when there was no tenure for teachers. Tenure has been a controversial issue for as long as I can remember. Like every other controversial issue there are positives and negatives. Some people see only the positives some only the negatives. Tenure came about for a reason. There are those who are concerned that eliminating it will bring back the negative conditions that were responsible for getting it started.

I have often heard it said that teachers stop performing once they get tenure. In fact, they continue to improve. In all my years as the principal of a school, I found very few who decided to perform at a lower level thinking they could get away with doing less once they attained tenure. They are sure that tenure will protect them. Firing a tenured teacher is difficult and should be made easier, but it certainly can be done.

13. Ducks and Eagles do not necessarily mix.

Closing failing schools and sending the students to other locations can be disruptive to both the sent and the receiving students. Instead, try reducing class size to twelve and keep them in the same, fixed up building.

Students learn far better in classes where they feel they are not just a number. With fewer students, individual learning problems can be spotted and addressed before the student just gives up or becomes a discipline problem. Parents who often fight to keep even a failing school open may be willing to help improve the school. Students will be kept busy doing work that enhances their learning. Teachers will be far more able to maintain control. We reduce class size for special needs students because we know that fewer students makes for fewer problems and better learning.

The visible cost of reducing class size to twelve is considerable. Additional teachers and classrooms are expensive! But so is failure! What does not having an employable skill cost a person? What does crime cost? What does prison cost? I wonder what the cost factor amounts to for the larger classes in schools designated as failing and are closed? Do kids sent to non-failing schools cause the new school to become a failing school? Is the cost for school drop-outs factored into the price?

We often hear how important educating the populace is to a democracy. If you, as I, believe this is true then let's start making the necessary changes that need to be made!

14. Last but not least, have a good time. Teaching is difficult but it can be a lot of fun. Teachers get a wonderful lift every time they realize they have made a difference in a student's life! Teachers have that opportunity frequently. Go for it! When you are having fun teaching, your students are having fun learning.

Epilogue

This book is meant to help those who teach to enjoy it more and be better at it. I hope it has!

Made in the USA
Middletown, DE
11 August 2023

36574752R00148